The Making of the Twentieth Century

This series of specially commissioned titles focuses attention on significant and often controversial events and themes of world history this century. The authors, many of them already outstanding in their field, have tried to close the gap between the intelligent layman, whose interest is aroused by recent history, and the specialist student at university. Each book will therefore provide sufficient narrative and explanation for the newcomer while offering the specialist student detailed source-references and bibliographies, together with interpretation and reassessment in the light of recent scholarship.

In the choice of subjects there will be a balance between breadth in some spheres and detail in others; between the essentially political and matters scientific, economic or social. The series cannot be a comprehensive account of everything that has happened in the twentieth century, but it will provide a guide to recent research and explain something of the times of extraordinary change and complexity in which we live.

The Making of the Twentieth Century

Series Editor: CHRISTOPHER THORNE

Other titles in the Series include

Already published

In preparation

Weimar and the Rise of Hitler

A. J. Nicholls

Macmillan

London · Melbourne · Toronto

St Martin's Press

New York

1 9 6 8

© A. J. Nicholls 1968

Published by
MACMILLAN AND CO LTD
Little Essex Street London WC2
and also at Bombay Calcutta and Madras
Macmillan South Africa (Publishers) Pty Ltd Johannesburg
The Macmillan Company of Australia Pty Ltd Melbourne
The Macmillan Company of Canada Ltd Toronto
St Martin's Press Inc New York

Library of Congress catalog card no. 68–29506

Printed in Great Britain by
ROBERT MACLEHOSE AND CO LTD
The University Press, Glasgow

TO

MY PARENTS

Contents

Plates and Maps

The cover pictures show Hitler rehearsing a speech before a mirror

PLATES

between pages 82 and 83

The author and publishers wish to thank the following for permission to reproduce the plates: Cover picture, 6, Zeitgeschichtliches Bildarchiv; 1*a*, Museum für Deutsche Geschichte; 1*b*, 4*c*, Staatsbibliothek Berlin Bildarchiv; 2, 3, 4*a* and *b*, 8*b*,

Radio Times Hulton Picture Library; 5, Suddeutscher Verlag
Bilderdienst; 7, Ullstein Bilderdienst; 8a, from *Satan in Top Hat*
by Tibor Koeves, Alliance Book Corporation, New York.

MAP

Abbreviations

BVP   *Bayerische Volkspartei* (Bavarian People's Party).

DDP   *Deutsche Demokratische Partei* (German Democratic Party).

DVP   *Deutsche Volkspartei* (German People's Party).

DNVP   *Deutschnationale Volkspartei* (German National People's Party – German Nationalists).

KPD   *Kommunistische Partei Deutschlands* (German Communist Party).

NSDAP   *Nationalsozialistische Deutsche Arbeiterpartei* (National Socialist German Workers' Party – Nazis).

SPD   *Sozialdemokratische Partei Deutschlands* (German Social Democratic Party – Majority Social Democrats).

USPD   *Unabhängige Sozialdemokratische Partei Deutschlands* (German Independent Social Democratic Party).

Preface

IN this book I have attempted to provide an introduction to the political history of the Weimar Republic. The failure of German democracy in the years after the First World War was of crucial importance, not only for Germany but for the world as a whole. It is necessary to understand the causes of this failure, and to avoid a natural tendency to over-simplify them. Very often they have been sought in the national character and historical development of the Germans, in the nature of Western capitalism, in the weaknesses of the Republican constitution or in the hypnotic power of Adolf Hitler. Some of these explanations are more respectable than others; none alone can begin to satisfy any serious enquiry.

One unforeseen by-product of Hitler's catastrophic war was the opening of German official records to historians. During the last two decades a great many valuable monographs have been published which throw light on the problems besetting the Weimar Republic. I have attempted to incorporate some of their findings into this book, but the need for compression precludes a detailed or definitive treatment. If I am able to stimulate the reader to delve more deeply into this fascinating and complicated subject I shall feel that my work has been justified.

My thanks are first of all due to my College for providing me with the facilities without which this book could not have been written. I should also like to acknowledge with gratitude the help I have received from Christopher Thorne and Miss Elizabeth Wiskemann. I am especially indebted to Sir John Wheeler-Bennett for his kindness in reading my manuscript and for his invaluable comments. I have

benefited greatly from discussions with my Oxford colleagues, especially Tim Mason, Jonathan Wright and
Modris Eksteins. Needless to say, I am entirely responsible
for the opinions expressed in the book and for any errors
which it may contain.

I wish to acknowledge the care and accuracy of
my typists, Miss D. Twamley and Miss E. Harrison, and
finally I should like to thank my wife for her constant
encouragement.

St. Antony's College   A. J. N.
Oxford
March 1968

Germany after the peace settlement

1 The Lost War

ON 29 September 1918 the German Army High Command advised its emperor, Kaiser Wilhelm II, that Germany must sue for peace. This marked a dramatic reversal of fortunes in the Great War. The previous spring had seen the launching of a massive German offensive on the Western Front. Its architect, General Ludendorff, had confidently predicted that it would bring the final triumph of German arms. Instead, by the autumn, German forces were in retreat and their allies defecting. Ludendorff and his titular superior, Field-Marshal Hindenburg, had to admit that military force alone could not save Germany.

Ludendorff recommended that the responsibility for negotiations should be laid on the shoulders of civilian politicians – who had had precious little influence on German policy since the summer of 1917. The government should also be given a wider and more popular character. It was hoped that this 'revolution from above' would appease public disaffection over a lost war.

Before the outbreak of hostilities in 1914 the German Empire had been a constitutional state with a democratically elected parliament (the Reichstag). Although the Kaiser's government was not appointed by the Reichstag and could not be held responsible to it in the manner of French or British governments, ministers needed the support of a parliamentary majority if they were to govern smoothly. Some of the parties on the left of the political spectrum – the Progressives and the large German Social Democratic Party – wanted an extension of parliamentary power. They hoped to see Germany's national government and local administration put under effective democratic control. In particular they wanted to reform the electoral system in Prussia, the largest state in the federal structure of the German Empire, where the right-wing parties were assured of predominant influence as the result of an unequal franchise. Generally speaking the same political elements were eager that Germany should pursue a foreign policy of international co-operation and peaceful development, although they were proud of their nation's achievements and were determined to further its interests.

On the other hand there were many powerful sectors of German society which felt that the Empire was not being assertive enough in the field of foreign affairs, that the liberal nature of Germany's political structure was a source of weakness, and that parliamentary government was a luxury which no nation as isolated and exposed as Germany could afford. These same critics of a liberal state also tended to be hostile to the growing urbanisation of their society, with the consequent expansion of a politically conscious working class. They disliked any form of cosmopolitan outlook.

Before 1914 the Imperial Government had usually looked for support in the Reichstag to one or other of the right-wing parties, the Conservatives or the National Liberals. The Centre Party, which represented the interests of the Roman Catholic minority in Germany, was at times persuaded to support the Government, but Roman Catholics were still regarded as outsiders by the Kaiser. As for the Social Democrats, the largest party in the Reichstag, they were politically detested as revolutionaries and socially unacceptable as members of an inferior class. It was true that the Social Democrats did have a revolutionary programme, but by 1914 their party had become far too accustomed to legality and peaceful agitation to desire a bloody confrontation with the ruling classes.

It was important in German life that political parties were regarded with distaste. Party intrigue was contrasted with the civil servant's sense of duty. Parliamentary squabbles were compared unfavourably with the loyalty and obedience of the Imperial Army. Many otherwise cultured and sophisticated Germans believed that there was something dirty about the business of politics. It was a belief by no means confined to Germany, but it was to have unfortunate consequences.

When the Great War broke out all the German parties rallied to their country's cause. Some of those on the left hoped that this would lead to political reforms. They were disappointed. Doubts also began to arise about the purely defensive nature of the war which Germany was waging, and there were fears that, if the Kaiser emerged victorious, his government would be encouraged to pursue a reactionary policy. This was particularly true after a political crisis in the summer of 1917, when the army leadership became the real voice of authority.

Some Social Democrats had always regretted their party's support for the war effort, and others soon joined them. In April 1917 the party split over this issue, and a minority broke away to form the Independent Social Democratic Party (USPD), dedicated to a rapid peace and the transformation of German society. On the left of the USPD there stood an even more radical group known as Spartakists, who wished to see extreme action taken against the Imperial régime. Its two most important leaders, Rosa Luxemburg and Karl Liebknecht, spent the last years of the war in prison.

On a less radical plane the Reichstag parties critical of the Imperial Government's conduct of the war began to consider how they could best improve the situation. In July 1917 an inter-party committee was set up to discuss means of pressing the Kaiser's ministers to adopt a more realistic view of Germany's military prospects. Two of the four parties represented on the committee, the SPD and the Progressives,* were also eager to build up a parliamentary majority to achieve political reforms.

* The others were the Centre and the National Liberals. The Independent Social Democrats were not in the committee.[1]

The committee continued to meet from time to time for the rest of the war, although the National Liberals left it towards the end of 1917. The zeal with which the parties pursued their aims of political reform and a negotiated peace waxed and waned according to the state of hostilities. But the habit of consultation between the leaders of the Social Democrats, Progressives and Centre seemed to foreshadow a political constellation which might become powerful if the Kaiser's military authorities lost their position of autocratic power.

Outside parliament the mood of the nation was gradually changing. The miseries and bereavements of the war affected the mass of the civilian population. A shortage of labour, horses and fertilisers was damaging the productivity of German farmers, while the temptations of the black market were more attractive than rigorously controlled sales supervised by the authorities. Urban workers were especially badly affected by food shortages, and their discontent manifested itself in occasional riots.

The morale of the army was similarly damaged by misery at home and prospects of an inglorious death at the front. In the battle area discipline still held, but camps and barracks inside Germany housed many soldiers who were substandard from the military viewpoint. Wounded, sick, temperamentally unsuited for front-line duty, or simply politically unreliable, these men acted as a disturbing leaven among the raw recruits training for their spell in the front line. State authorities were not well placed to combat serious internal unrest. Police forces were depleted owing to the war. The best officers and NCOs were at the front. Nor was co-operation between the civilian and military authorities always of the most effective nature.

The domestic background was not, therefore, very reassuring when Hindenburg and Ludendorff decided that Germany must seek an armistice. It was, indeed, to be an armistice of a very one-sided character, since it would enable

their armies to withdraw unscathed to the German frontier
and stay there in a defensive posture.

Ludendorff knew very well that the Allies would be
unlikely to accept his conditions. When one of his staff
officers asked him if he would agree to a truce if he were
Marshal Foch* he replied, 'Of course not, I should press on
hard. But perhaps this offer will not be unwelcome to him.
In war one can never be sure.'[2] Ludendorff himself admitted
he was grasping at a straw. As for the reorganisation of the
Government, his motives were a mixture of calculation and
spite. On the one hand he was genuinely concerned with the
problem of maintaining order at home so that the army
could be held together. On the other he loathed reformist
politicians and wanted to saddle them with the responsibility for defeat. On 1 October he told his commanders that
those people should be brought into the Government 'whom
we have to thank for bringing us to this pass. We shall
therefore see these gentlemen come into the Ministry. They
must make the peace that has now to be concluded. They
must now eat the dish which they have prepared for us.'
It was small wonder that the colonel who recorded these
words was reminded of Siegfried, mortally wounded by
Hagen's spear plunged in his back.[3] It is in the nature of
men to blame others for their own mistakes and Ludendorff
was no exception. For him the German collapse had been
caused by weakness and conspiracy at home. The army was
blameless. It was the beginning of a legend which was to
haunt Germany until 1945, when the Red Army stood
triumphant in the ruins of Berlin.

Ludendorff's sudden urge to create a parliamentary
régime ran parallel with the efforts which some members of
the Reichstag majority – especially the Progressives and
Social Democrats – had been making to build up resistance
against the Imperial authorities' handling of the situation
and at last impose parliamentary government on the

* The Allied commander-in-chief.

Empire. The Inter-Fractional Committee of the Reichstag had been keeping itself informed as far as was possible about the war situation, and the leaders of the Social Democratic, Progressive and Centre Parties were aware that the position was grave. They thought, however, that enough time would be granted to Germany to negotiate an acceptable peace if a government which enjoyed their confidence could be created. Their efforts were forestalled by Ludendorff's volte-face. Instead of Germany receiving a parliamentary régime as the result of Reichstag pressure she apparently obtained it by the grace of the High Command.

The man selected to be Chancellor in the new government was Prince Max of Baden. He was the protégé of the Progressive Party leader Haussmann, who thought that he combined sound ideas with the social prestige necessary to withstand pressure from the army.[4] Prince Max had no desire to be responsible for a sudden armistice offer, since this would damage public morale and might lead to the accusation that politicians were betraying the army. He knew that, unless he was cautious, he might find himself the object of a favourite German saying, 'The pen has thrown away what the sword has won'.[5] He therefore urged that a more general offer of peace be made before a specific appeal for an armistice, and refused to transmit such an appeal until a ministry had been formed. His new government was to be of a much more democratic character than previous Imperial administrations. The decision to widen the basis of the ministry meant that leaders of the parliamentary parties had to be told of the military crisis. Many of them were shocked and astonished.

This shock had its effect on the so-called 'parliamentarisation' which was supposed to accompany Prince Max's elevation to the Chancellorship. It was quite clear that this was a death-bed conversion so far as the Kaiser and the High Command were concerned. The parties which had been most eager for constitutional changes – the Social

Democrats, the Progressives and the Centre Party – had not won them by asserting their own parliamentary influence. They owed them to Germany's foes. An invitation to enter the Government at that stage was an invitation to share in the greatest humiliation ever inflicted on Germany. Many Social Democrats would have preferred to decline it. The fact that the new Reich Chancellor was a prince and a major-general hardly made the government more attractive from their viewpoint. But their leader, Friedrich Ebert, was convinced that his party should not refuse to serve. It ought not to be said of the Social Democrats that they left their country in the lurch in its darkest hour. Ebert was a sincere patriot, as were most of his colleagues. He had not wanted to betray his country in 1914, and he would not weaken now.

By participating in the Government the Majority Social Democrats lost the chance of steering the growing anti-war movement for their own purposes. The Independent Social Democrats were quick to accuse them of bolstering up a rotten régime which ought to be allowed to collapse.

As the month of October wore on and peace was not concluded, popular hostility to the nation's leadership grew more intense. On 24 October the representative of the Saxon government in Berlin reported:

Two moods are predominant among the masses. The first is a yearning for peace which has now grown to an extreme pitch. The second is an unmistakable bitterness over the fact that previous governments did not recognize the limits of German strength but went on nourishing the belief in Germany's invincibility so effectively that broad circles of the population were lulled into a sense of false security. . . .[6]

With victory clearly impossible, public opinion swung behind those demanding immediate peace. If the institutions of the Empire were obstacles to that demand they would have to be eliminated.

The internal crisis had been directly affected by the course of the armistice negotiations. Prince Max was finally prevailed upon to issue an appeal to President Wilson, and from the answers received it became clear, not only that the Western Allies would insist on the elimination of Germany's capacity to continue the war, but also that the Kaiser himself was a major obstacle to peace.

An American Note of 14 October spoke of the need to destroy those forces in Germany which threatened the peace of the world. Nine days later the message was made more explicit.

By 31 October external pressure for abdication had become so intense that the cabinet was forced to discuss the matter very seriously. The Social Democratic spokesman at the meeting, Philipp Scheidemann, urged that the Kaiser should be asked to abdicate. This was a wise proposal, but no decision was taken. Wilhelm II remained where he was.[7]

It was at this juncture that discipline in the armed services began to break down. The trouble started among naval units in Kiel and Wilhelmshaven. Since the battle of Jutland in 1916 the German High Seas Fleet had been virtually confined to the North Sea ports as a defensive screen for U-boat warfare. On 28 October it was ordered to sea for a major operation in the English Channel.

The German naval staff was determined that hostilities should not be allowed to end without an impressive action by their fleet. They wanted to be sure that the German navy would outlive the war. They did not fully explain the significance of their plans to the German government, even though the operation might well have prejudiced the armistice negotiations then in progress.[8] As it happened, the naval chiefs were thwarted by opposition from their own ranks.

The sailors, among whom resentment at harsh discipline and enforced idleness had already found expression in mutinous outbreaks, refused to obey orders. Attempts to punish them led to demonstrations. Troops were called out to restore the situation, but proved unreliable. After some bloodshed the authorities wavered. Their position was usurped by a committee of rebellious soldiers and sailors. Red flags were hoisted. The German revolution had begun.

Full details of the titles and articles cited in the references can be found in the Bibliography, pp. 179 ff.

[1] See Matthias, *Der Interfraktionelle Ausschuss*, vol. I, pp. xxxiii–iv.

[2] *Ursachen und Folgen. Vom deutschen Zusammenbruch 1918 und 1945 bis zur staatlichen Neuordnung Deutschlands in der Gegenwart* (eds. Michaelis–Schraepler–Scheel), vol. II, p. 324. Hereafter cited as *Ursachen und Folgen*.

[3] Ibid. pp. 322–4.

[4] Matthias–Morsey, *Die Regierung des Prinzen Max von Baden*, pp. xxii–ix. Also Robson, 'Left-Wing Liberalism in Germany, 1900–1919' (unpublished D.Phil. thesis, Oxford, 1966) p. 350.

[5] *Ursachen und Folgen*, vol. II, p. 327.

[6] Cited in Kolb, *Arbeiterräte*, pp. 18–19.

[7] Burdick–Lutz, *Political Institutions*, p. 27.

[8] For a discussion of the German navy's attitude towards the operations at the end of October see Deist, 'Seekriegsleitung und Flotten-rebellion', *Vierteljahrshefte für Zeitgeschichte*, Oct. 1966, pp. 341 ff.

2 The German Revolution

THE Kiel mutiny was the first of a chain of revolts which spread across Germany in the next few days and which finally disrupted the German Empire. It is common to stress their unpolitical nature. More than one German historian has pointed out that dissidents in the armed forces hoisted the Red Flag because it was the only banner under which they could be sure of evading punishment for their action. Strikers or demonstrators could hope for reform; mutineers had to opt for revolution.[1]

Certainly the left-wing political parties were ill-prepared when revolution came. The SPD, although it had put peace and democratic reform in the forefront of its programme, wanted no violent upheaval, and would have been happy to accept a constitutional monarchy. The Independent Socialists were more willing to exploit mass unrest in their campaign for an immediate end to the war. Some of them worked together with radical elements among the factory workers in Berlin and other large cities to further revolutionary agitation. But they did not really imagine that the powerful machinery of the German State would be vulnerable to working-class assault for many months. The same view was held by the leaders of the truly revolutionary pressure group on the left of the USPD, the *Gruppe Internationale* or Spartakists. Most of the Spartakist militants were, in any case, under some sort of official restraint in October 1918. It was the sudden demoralisation created within Germany by the news of impending defeat which paralysed the repressive forces of the old order and conditioned the masses to accept a major political change.

Nevertheless, the revolution did not take place by accident. Despite a great deal of repression the Independents had been agitating in Germany for an end to hostilities, the freeing of political prisoners, an end to restrictions on public expression, better food and working conditions and really democratic government. In the context of Germany in 1918 this was a revolutionary programme, and many members of the more militant element in the USPD were willing to recognise it as such. There was, indeed, confusion in the party's rank and file about how far revolution should be designed to end the war and how far agitation to end the war should be exploited to create a revolution. Most of the more prominent members of the USPD – for example, Hugo Haase and Karl Kautsky – were more interested in peace than revolution. But in Berlin groups of radical factory shop stewards and militant members of the Independent Socialist youth group were less moderately inclined.

Many of the unknown and obscure men who took the lead at crucial moments in the German revolution had been exposed to Independent Social Democratic propaganda or had themselves actually been involved in subversive political activity. At Kiel, for example, the sailors could remember the harsh sentences meted out to leaders of an earlier – and very restrained – political manifestation, in which some of the accused had admitted links with the Independent Social Democratic Party.[2]

The soldiers in rear areas played a key role in overthrowing the German Empire. They alone could have suppressed the revolutionary movement. In fact they were more affected by anti-war feeling than almost any other section of the population. There were, of course, many troops who had no political views and no inclination to revolt, but they saw little sense in shooting their countrymen just to continue a war that had already been lost. The rank and file of obedient soldiers upon whom authority depended had only one overwhelming desire: to go home.

A broad pattern of revolution began to make itself apparent. Mass meetings in favour of peace and political reform would be held, followed by marches and demonstrations. Soldiers and sailors usually made up the most radical element in these activities, and were in the vanguard of any riotous outbreaks which developed from them. The police and military would try to ban such manifestations, but would find they had no power to enforce restrictions. Official retreats encouraged more daring action by the demonstrators. Majority Socialist leaders usually tried to gain control of the crowds and prevent them from transgressing the bounds of peaceful demonstration, and sometimes they were successful. But in other cases more zealous agitators – sometimes members of the USPD – would lead the crowds to barracks, prisons or government offices. Soldiers would be disarmed and persuaded to join the revolution. Political prisoners were released. Municipal and, in some cases, governmental authority was taken over by the rebels. Revolutionary power would be exercised by so-called 'workers' and soldiers' councils' or 'Soviets'.

These bodies undoubtedly owed their conception to the Russian revolution, but there was great vagueness about their precise form and function. Few Germans had a very clear idea of what was happening in Russia. In any case, the behaviour of the Bolsheviks had aroused strong criticism throughout the German Labour movement, and not least in the USPD. So far as the purpose of the workers' and soldiers' councils was concerned confusion reigned within both the socialist parties, but it was most marked among the Independents. For the most part the Majority Socialists tended to see the councils simply as devices to maintain law and order in a turbulent situation. They hoped that they would quickly disappear. Many of the Independents had more ambitious plans, wanting to use the councils as organs of working-class self-expression which could draw the masses into political activity in a manner impossible with a more conventional parliamentary constitution. They could also be used to create genuinely democratic institutions in Germany before any more formal decisions were taken by an elected parliament. Such a development could be carried into the social field, and many Independents thought that initial steps towards the socialisation of Germany's economy should be taken by the councils without waiting for any parliamentary sanction. Lastly there were those who felt that the councils should be instruments of proletarian dictatorship which would replace bourgeois parliaments altogether. In November 1918 their numbers were quite insignificant.[3]

During the first few days after the Kiel disturbances power had changed hands in only a few north-western cities and only on a local level. But on 7 November a more serious event took place. In Munich, the capital of Bavaria, a by-election campaign had been transformed into a determined agitation for a German Republic. Faced with a complete breakdown of police and military authority, the last of the Wittelsbach kings, the aged Ludwig III, left his palace in the middle of the night and never returned to it. On the following day it was announced that Bavaria was a Republic. Its new premier was an Independent Social Democrat, Kurt Eisner, who had only recently been released from prison.[4]

With this blow at the monarchical system the fate of the German Empire was really sealed. The Majority Socialists could not afford to let the Independents take the lead in winning power. They had to act quickly if their party was to control events in the future.

The situation in Berlin had been deteriorating, although it was not yet so desperate as in cities to the west and south. A group of factory shop stewards in the capital's heavy industrial plants were preparing for a revolution to take place on 11 November.[5] Workers' and Soldiers' Councils

were being set up, despite the express prohibition of the
Army High Command. The Majority Social Democrats
had managed to prevent any serious outburst among
Berlin's factory workers, but by 7 November the party felt
it could wait no longer. An ultimatum was presented to the
cabinet; if the Kaiser and the Crown Prince did not
abdicate within two days the SPD would leave the coalition.

On the morning of 9 November Prince Max announced
the Kaiser's abdication and handed over his post as Reich
Chancellor to Friedrich Ebert. At the same time Ebert
offered equal participation in his new government to the
Independent Social Democrats.

It was too late to save the monarchy. As the day wore on
large crowds of soldiers and workers marched on the
government buildings in the centre of the city. It became
known that Karl Liebknecht was about to proclaim a
German Republic. Once again the danger loomed that the
SPD would lose command of events to a really radical group.
Faced with this situation Scheidemann went to a window of
the Reichstag building and announced to the cheering
spectators below that Germany had become a Republic.
The Wilhelmine Empire was at an end.[6]

That same day the Kaiser, having refused to abdicate
while there was still time to save his dynasty, followed the
advice of his Army Chief of Staff, General Groener, and left
Germany for Holland. He had had no choice in the matter.
It had become obvious that Germany's soldiers would not
fight their comrades to save the Hohenzollerns.

The Social Democrats had not wanted a Republic. Ebert
felt that discontented royalists might weaken the State for
years to come.[7] All the gains that his party hoped for could
have been settled within a constitutional monarchy. Even
the new National Assembly, which was to replace the old
Reichstag, had been suggested by Prince Max before the
Kaiser abdicated. Ebert was also deeply concerned about
the effect which chaos in Germany might have on the

conduct of peace negotiations. On the morning of 10 November the Imperial cabinet met for the last time. Ebert took the chair as Chancellor. A German armistice commission under Erzberger had already gone to negotiate with the Western Allies, and had relayed the conditions to be imposed upon the German armed forces back to Berlin. Ebert told his colleagues:

There is no alternative to accepting the armistice terms. It is, however, already apparent that these conditions will not produce a just peace. The sacrifices imposed on us are tremendous, they must lead to our people's doom.[8]

Germany's representatives signed the armistice on the following day, and hostilities ceased. But Ebert was haunted by the fear that a collapse of military discipline or public order in Germany might bring Entente troops across the Rhine. Reports from German embassies in neutral countries suggested that if any sign of Bolshevism appeared in Germany an invasion might follow.[9]

It was not a situation in which to embark on political experiments. However, now that the Republic had come Ebert and his colleagues had to make the best of it. They set about their task with a determination not equalled among their Independent Socialist rivals.

Real power in Berlin rested at that moment with the Workers' and Soldiers' Councils. The Majority Social Democrats conducted vigorous propaganda to ensure that delegates sympathetic to them were elected to these. The SPD speakers were more experienced than their rivals and were often better known. Most of those voting for the councils did not think that there ought to be a split in the socialist ranks at that moment. Ebert also persuaded the leadership of the Independent Social Democratic Party – which was very confused about its aims now that the revolution had actually broken out – to co-operate with him in forming a government.

When a meeting of Berlin Workers' and Soldiers' Councils was held on 10 November it sanctioned a ruling cabinet of six – three Majority Social Democrats and three Independents. Ebert was chairman.

An Executive Committee of the Workers' and Soldiers' Councils in Berlin was also set up, but its functions were left vague and an attempt to prevent the Majority Social Democrats receiving representation on it was thwarted. It was true that the new government was called a 'Council of People's Representatives', but the name was not of great importance. To all intents and purposes, Ebert remained Reich Chancellor.

The new revolutionary government was an uneasy but not impossible coalition. Its three Social Democratic members, Ebert, Scheidemann and Landsberg, were eager to re-establish order in Germany and to organise the election of a National Assembly. Once these objectives were gained it would be possible to negotiate a Peace Treaty with the Entente and set about the reconstruction of Germany's economic life. They assumed that democratic elections would produce a very powerful socialist group in the new National Assembly. They had no reason to believe that the sort of Germany they wanted could not be created with the aid of existing bureaucratic institutions, especially since they had themselves been drawn into the Imperial Government before the revolution had broken out.

Their leader, Friedrich Ebert, was forty-nine years old, the son of a master tailor in Heidelberg. A fine organiser, he had made his career in the administrative machine of the Social Democratic Party. It had been thanks to men of his stamp that the party had been able to build up its membership and electoral support so successfully before 1914. He was skilled in the arts of negotiation and conciliation, but could on occasion give way to bursts of temperament.[10] Ebert was at any rate a man of strong and determined will. In him the SPD possessed a clear-headed leader, but one whose mental horizons were narrow.

The Independents were not such a closely-knit group as their SPD colleagues. By far the most radical was Emil Barth, who had been collecting arms for a revolution since the beginning of 1918.[11] The others, Hugo Haase and Wilhelm Dittmann, were of a different stamp. Both had been Reichstag deputies in 1914 and were therefore old colleagues of the Majority Social Democrats. On the face of it there was no clear reason why the two sections of the socialist cabinet should not work together. Now that the war was over the main objective of the USPD had apparently been achieved. Certainly there was no thought of a Red dictatorship on the Russian model.

It soon turned out, however, that the difficulties in the way of socialist co-operation were very formidable. The personal rancour created by the split in the German Labour movement during the war was not easily forgotten. The SPD leaders had been associated with the war effort, and had finally been taken into the government. The Independents had been ostracised as subversives or even traitors. Some of them had suffered imprisonment; many had committed illegal acts. They, in turn, regarded the collaborationist attitude of the SPD as a betrayal of socialist principles.

Then there were differences about the way in which the revolution ought to be exploited. Mindful of his country's military situation, Ebert wanted to end disorders in Germany as soon as possible and call elections to a National Assembly. The Independents saw the events of 9 November as a victory, and the end of the war as a heroic achievement. They did not want a Soviet dictatorship, but they did believe German society ought to be fundamentally altered. Before a National Assembly was elected they thought that the country should be given time to adjust itself to the revolution. In particular, the working classes should be

mobilised for political action through the agency of the
Workers' and Soldiers' Councils.

The Independents also wanted immediate steps taken
towards socialising large-scale industry, whereas Ebert and
his colleagues wanted such decisions left to the National
Assembly. The German trade union organisation was
negotiating an industrial bargaining agreement with
employers and did not wish to see this undermined by
'excesses' on the part of the Workers' Councils. The
Independents argued that, unless radical change was
carried through as part of the revolution, it might never
come at all. Time was to prove them right.

If personal experience and policies divided the SPD from
their coalition partners, their relations with the officials of
the old Empire deepened the cleavage between them. The
bureaucrats in the Reich Ministries behaved as though
Ebert – officially only the chairman of a governing committee – were an old-style Reich Chancellor. His instructions were treated as binding orders, whereas Independent
Socialist members of the Committee found their directives
being referred to him for ratification. The agenda of
cabinet meetings was drawn up by Ebert and he led the
discussions. The division of labour on the committee also
meant that the SPD members had the most important tasks
allotted to them.[12]

The immediate problems which faced the People's Commissioners were the re-establishment of government authority throughout Germany and the evacuation of German
troops from all areas west of the Rhine. The latter was a condition of the armistice and had to be fulfilled if Germany
was to avoid invasion. Both issues involved delicate relationships with the Workers' and Soldiers' Councils, and in particular with the executive committee established in Berlin.

This committee claimed that Ebert and the other People's
Representatives were only functioning with its consent, and
implied that if they did not rule according to its wishes they

could be replaced. In order to ensure that revolutionary influence prevailed in Berlin it tried to set up a 'Red Guard'. It also encouraged Workers' and Soldiers' Councils to try and exercise control over civil servants and municipal officials. In both these enterprises it failed miserably. The Soldiers' Councils themselves opposed any force in Berlin which might rival their own.[13] The authority of German officialdom proved too great for the Workers' Councils. Generally speaking, they were unable to exercise any real control over internal administration.

When the committee convened a National Congress of German Workers' and Soldiers' Councils in Berlin on 16 December the result was a triumph for Ebert. The Congress voted in favour of rapid elections for a national constituent assembly. A Central Committee was set up dominated by Majority Social Democrats. Attempts by the Congress to press socialisation and army reform on the Government were evaded by procrastination and technical objections.

Despite the failures of the Executive Committee, Ebert's government was still faced with the problem of organising an effective armed force to protect itself. The Soldiers' Councils had real power among the troops in Berlin. Yet these could not be used as the foundation for a Republican army. They were far too concerned with undermining the authority of their superiors. In any case, many units were beginning to break up. By the middle of December the army was in dissolution. Those who remained in the barracks did so as much to obtain food and shelter as to act as defenders of the new régime. Indeed some of them, like Adolf Hitler in Munich, were disgusted with the collapse of their old, proud regiments and blamed the revolution for their humiliation.

For Ebert the problem of maintaining order and discipline in the army seemed far more serious than the need to build up new contingents loyal to socialism or the Republic. His views on the military situation were, therefore, very similar

B

to those held by the old Imperial High Command. General Groener, who had tackled the unenviable task of advising the Kaiser to leave Germany, was the most intelligent and effective leader of the old officer corps. Groener had got in touch with Ebert soon after the Republic had been pro-claimed. A private wire linked the High Command to the Reich Chancellery and consultations between the two men could be conducted without difficulty. Ebert did not publicise his contacts with Groener, but he saw nothing wrong in them. The High Command offered to co-operate with the Republican government if it in turn was prepared to maintain discipline in the armed forces. This was entirely consistent with Ebert's programme. Groener seemed at that time to be in a weak position *vis-à-vis* the socialist politicians, since he needed their help to maintain his position.

For the time being Groener and his nominal superior, Field-Marshal Hindenburg, wanted above all to prevent revolutionary disaffection spreading to the soldiers on the front in the west. They calculated, quite correctly, that these forces would be willing to be led home by their officers without mutinous disturbance. Soldiers' Councils among the field army units were later established under the supervision of officers and were usually loyal to them. Once in Germany, it was hoped, the Front Army would provide both the officer corps and the Government with a reliable force with which to stabilise an apparently insecure situa-tion. This proposition was just as attractive to Ebert as it was to the officer corps.[14] The executive committee of the Berlin Workers' and Soldiers' Councils did not know of these arrangements between Groener and Ebert, but they suspected quite rightly that the SPD leaders had a very different view of the army's future from their own.

There is no doubt that more could have been done to create an armed force that was emotionally loyal to the Republic. In December 1918 the old army was in ruins, and Groener was unable to offer the Government effective protection. The administration of military affairs was under the control of the Prussian War Ministry, and the Independent Social Democrats in the Government urged that an officer known to approve of the revolution be appointed as its head. Ebert passed over their suggestion. He preferred Colonel Reinhardt, who described himself as a 'convinced monarchist, but one who would never use the troops entrusted to him to attack the government'.[15]

It was small wonder that many of the Independent Social Democrats and their supporters in the Workers' and Soldiers' Councils took the view that Ebert was giving way to counter-revolutionary pressure. Their fears were increased by a virulent press campaign against the more radical revolutionaries and the 'excesses' of the councils.

When a conflict occurred between the Majority Socialist leaders and a mutinous unit of sailors quartered in the centre of Berlin the Independents decided to resign from the Government. They did so on 27 December. Ebert and his colleagues carried on alone.

They faced a tense situation made worse by Germany's economic difficulties. War production naturally fell away with the end of hostilities. At the same time men returning from the front demanded jobs. Industry was very short of raw materials, and the fact that the Allies maintained their blockade of Germany even after the armistice had been signed did not facilitate a resumption of peacetime production. Germany was, in any case, cut off from most of her pre-war export markets. Unemployment, especially in big towns like Berlin and Munich, began to become a serious problem. The Spartakists and radical Independents did their best to mobilise support among unemployed workers.

The radical shop stewards and the left wing of the Independent Social Democrats were now totally opposed to Ebert's government and determined to resist it through the medium of the Workers' and Soldiers' Councils. Their influence in the USPD was growing and divisions between them and more moderate elements were becoming very serious. The most consistent radical voices on the left belonged to the Spartakist Union, whose leaders, Rosa Luxemburg and Karl Liebknecht, argued that the November revolution was a sham and that the proletariat must be mobilised to take over power itself. On 31 December the Spartakists held a Congress at which it was decided to break away from the Independents and form a separate German Communist Party. The radical shop-stewards in Berlin considered joining the new party, but no satisfactory terms could be worked out for them. Under the leadership of Rosa Luxemburg the party seemed likely to follow an independent course, even though Karl Radek, a Bolshevik agent of Lenin, had been present at the foundation Congress.[16]

The language of the German Communists, as expressed at meetings and in their paper *Die Rote Fahne* (The Red Flag), was very violent and seemed to be encouraging immediate insurrection. Actually Rosa Luxemburg saw it as the party's task to educate the German masses by demonstrating the conservative nature of the Ebert government. Only then, in her view, would they be roused to demand revolutionary action. Until that mass support was available she and Karl Liebknecht had no desire to initiate a *coup*. But many of their supporters were less sophisticated. They were eager to risk a conflict while Berlin was still in an atmosphere of turmoil.

Its occasion was the dismissal from office of Emil Eichhorn, a left-wing Independent Social Democrat who held the post of Police President in Berlin. He refused to make way, and large-scale demonstrations took place in his favour. The Independent Social Democrats, radical shop-stewards and Communists who provoked these demonstrations were carried away with enthusiasm at their success. They established a revolutionary committee and declared Ebert's government deposed. Fighting broke out.

The German revolution seemed about to enter a new and more extreme phase.

In fact the 'Spartakist rising', as it later became known, was virtually unplanned and chaotic in execution. Although Rosa Luxemburg's Communist (Spartakist) Party was identified with the rising in government propaganda, Rosa Luxemburg herself had not thought that the time was ripe for such a move. Once fighting had started, however, she believed that the workers' leaders ought not to desert them or encourage them to surrender.[17] Her party reaped the benefits of repression, notoriety and martyrdom. For the German Labour movement as a whole the fighting brought nothing but tragedy.

Most of the rank and file in both Social Democratic Parties in Berlin wanted to avoid fraternal conflict. It is possible that a determined effort by Ebert and his colleagues to negotiate with the Independents and the radical shop stewards might have led to a compromise.[18] But this would have implied that the Government could not assert its authority in Berlin. Negotiations with the USPD would also have involved taking steps to create a more genuinely revolutionary administration, particularly in the fields of military organisation and police. Ebert was not the man to risk the chaos which such doubtful experiments might bring with them. In view of Germany's desperate situation and the complete confusion of the German radical left, it is hard to condemn him. Nevertheless, the effects of his actions were unhappy for the future of the Republic.

The rebels were crushed after some bitter fighting. The new Defence Minister in Ebert's government, Gustav Noske, made use of volunteer units raised by the old Army Command and paid by the Prussian War Ministry. These *Freikorps* formations were led by Imperial officers, most of whom were violently opposed to the revolution. On 15 January Rosa Luxemburg and Karl Liebknecht were murdered by officers and men in one of these units. Their killing was a brutal and unnecessary crime carried out by politically ignorant men. Noske became regarded on the left as the butcher of his class.

This was not the only atrocity to besmirch Republican arms in 1919, and most victims of such violence were men of the left. Noske's forces freed Berlin from the fear of a Communist insurrection, but at the expense of working-class unity. The damage done to the German Labour movement by its early experiences in the revolution was never repaired. Proletarian solidarity remained an empty slogan until Hitler subjected all German workers to the control of the Nazi Labour Front.

On 19 January the Social Democrats lost their monopoly of German political life. In the elections for the National Assembly both socialist parties put together were in a minority. The tide of the German revolution had turned. Its ebb was to be a rapid one.

The revolution has often been described as a failure. In the sense that it did not bring socialism to Germany this is true. Yet it may be doubted whether the German people were prepared to accept large-scale social experiments in 1918. Certainly those who urged radical measures were very confused in both their aims and methods. The organs of working-class self-expression, the Workers' and Soldiers' Councils, could not assert themselves against experienced labour leaders and civil servants.

On the other hand, the revolution had provided Germany with an armistice and a Republic. It was clear that her new political institutions would be genuinely democratic in a sense they had never been before. Pressure from outside parliament had achieved a greater degree of parliamentaris-ation than had been possible under the Empire. The reform movement within the former Reichstag had never looked strong enough to assert itself against the Imperial régime – the revolution had toppled that régime altogether. Germany had not been transformed. Yet, the new Republic promised to be a freer and more egalitarian State than its Imperial predecessor.

[1] For instance, Rosenberg, *Geschichte der deutschen Republik* (Karlsbad, 1935) pp. 13–14. Also Heiber, *Republik von Weimar*, p. 14.

[2] See, for example, the statements made in Wilhelmshaven by the sailors Reichpeitsch and Kolbis in August 1917. *Ursachen und Folgen*, vol. I, p. 228.

[3] For a discussion of German attitudes towards the Workers' and Soldiers' Councils, see Tormin, *Rätediktatur und Soziale Demokratie*, pp. 26–52.

[4] The best account of these events in English is in Mitchell's *Revolution in Bavaria, 1918–1919*.

[5] Kolb, *Arbeiterräte*, pp. 42, 62, citing Müller, *Vom Kaiserreich zur Republik*, vol. I, p. 139. See also Barth, *Aus der Werkstatt der deutschen Revolution*, pp. 49–51.

[6] Scheidemann, *The Making of the New Germany*, vol. II, pp. 261–4.

[7] Eyck, *History of the Weimar Republic*, vol. I, p. 45.

[8] Burdick–Lutz, *Political Institutions*, p. 39.

[9] Ibid. p. 70.

[10] Kotowski, *Friedrich Ebert*, pp. 154–6.

[11] Barth, *Werkstatt*, pp. 24 ff.

[12] Kolb, *Arbeiterräte*, p. 123.

[13] Burdick–Lutz, *Political Institutions*, p. 48; also *Ursachen und Folgen*, vol. III, p. 13.

[14] For a discussion of the hopes the High Command placed in the front army and its attitude to Soldiers' Councils see Carsten, *Reichswehr*, pp. 7–12. Also Gordon, *The Reichswehr*, p. 9.

[15] Burdick–Lutz, *Political Institutions*, p. 166.

[16] For details of this congress see Waldmann, *Spartakist Rising*, pp. 149–58. Also Flechtheim, *Kommunistische Partei*, pp. 45–7; Angress, *Stillborn Revolution*, pp. 23–7; Nettl, *Rosa Luxemburg*, vol. II, pp. 753–61.

[17] For a fuller discussion of the complex motives and often contradictory behaviour within the Communist Party at this time see Nettl, *Rosa Luxemburg*, pp. 761–8.

[18] See, for example, Kolb, *Arbeiterräte*, p. 239.

3 The Foundations of the New Republic

To most Germans the defeat of the Spartakist rising seemed to be a victory for moderation and legality. Ebert, who personified both these qualities, achieved another important objective on 19 January, when Germany went to the polls to elect a Constituent National Assembly. The elections were held in an atmosphere of crisis. Their smooth completion was a triumph for the Republican government. For the first time all adult Germans of both sexes were voting for a truly powerful representative body.

Return to constitutional forms gave Germany's non-socialist parties a chance to assert themselves for the first time since the revolution. From Ebert's point of view, this was quite a healthy development. He had asked Haussmann, the Progressive Party leader, to stay in his government in November 1918. Although this had proved impossible, the collaboration between Majority Social Democrats and the other parties of the old Reichstag majority – Centre and Progressives – might well be revived in the new Republic.

Changes which had taken place in the old Reichstag parties since the the revolution had apparently made such collaboration more likely. The Progressives – who had always been in favour of genuine parliamentary government – swung sharply to the left and merged into a new party, the Democrats. This had been founded by a group of intellectuals, journalists and businessmen who felt that the old liberalism had not been decisive or bold enough to make an impression on German Society. The majority of the Progressive Party was persuaded to join it, giving the Democrats a political machine with which to fight the elections. Very soon Progressives began to dominate the party.[1] At the same time negotiations were going on between the Progressives and the more right-wing National Liberals, whose members had been badly shaken by the collapse of the Empire.

For a moment it looked as though the forces of German liberalism – which had been split since the time of Bismarck – would unite on a platform of Republican democracy. That this did not happen was due initially to the overconfidence of the new Democratic leaders who refused to give the old National Liberals adequate status in the new organisation. Although some of the National Liberals swallowed unfavourable terms and joined the new party, others remained outside.

They were rallied by Gustav Stresemann, the most energetic National Liberal leader, whose Pan-German record in the war had made him unpalatable to the Democrats. At a meeting of the National Liberal Executive attended by only a fraction of those eligible, Stresemann was able to gain a slender majority for the merger of the party into an organisation of his own called the German People's Party (DVP).[2] Later on a good deal of attention was paid to this failure to achieve liberal unity, and Stresemann's part in it received particular scrutiny. At the time he did not seem nearly so important, especially to the triumphant Democrats.[3] In any case it is very doubtful if a real chance of lasting union was cast aside in December 1918. The revolution had frightened many of the old guard into accepting a programme of complete democracy and social reform, but once normality returned their natural aversion for socialism and the Republic asserted itself.

For the time being Stresemann's People's Party remained weak in numbers and organisation. Its programme was vague and ambivalent, since its candidates sometimes adopted a moderately Republican pose and sometimes revealed themselves as monarchists. In fact, Stresemann and his followers were still attached to the monarchy, and wished to combat the threat of socialist legislation against the propertied classes.[4]

The Democrats, on the other hand, enthusiastically committed themselves to the Republic, and to a programme of democratic reform. For many of them, however, the revolution in November had been a bitter pill to swallow. The Progressives had seen in Prince Max's government the achievement of their political goal; the peaceful and orderly democratisation of Germany. The revolution had upset this development and threatened the country with anarchy. It had also forced the Social Democrats to adopt a more radical posture just at the moment when they seemed ready to co-operate most effectively with the middle-class parties.[5]

The Roman Catholic Centre Party had not welcomed the revolution. Even before it had broken out the Centre had been divided in its attitude towards Prince Max's government. The collapse of the Empire took the Centre completely by surprise. Its leaders reacted with astonishment and dismay. Trimborn, president of the party's Rhineland section, voiced a general feeling when he described the revolution as a 'national disaster'. There was great confusion about the way in which the party should react to the new situation. Most of its functionaries were loyal to the Empire, but the trade union wing of the party – important in the western provinces of Germany – wanted to exploit the revolution to gain social reforms. There was a real danger that the Centre would disintegrate. Salvation came from an unlikely quarter. The new socialist government in Prussia included Adolf Hoffmann, an Independent Social Democrat, as Education Minister. Hoffmann was eager to free education from clerical influence. So great was the furore aroused by his plans to secularise schools that the Centre in Prussia rallied its forces to oppose him. Defence of Roman Catholic rights once more became a political issue,

and it restored the wavering unity of the socially hetero-
geneous Centre Party.[6]

The last important group to contest the election stood
uncompromisingly, if somewhat nervously, on the right.
This was the German National People's Party or DNVP.
The DNVP was a coalition of conservative and right-radical
groups represented in the old Reichstag. The major conservative party, the DKP, which had drawn a good deal of
its strength from the landed interests in Germany's eastern
provinces, put its electoral machine at the disposal of the
DNVP. Nevertheless many old conservative leaders were
forced to play a relatively inconspicuous role in the new
organisation because it was feared that the electorate would
reject such obviously backward-looking social elements.[7]
Although more than a quarter of the DNVP's elected
representatives in the National Assembly were returned in
the provinces of East and West Prussia, Posen and
Pomerania,[8] the party was not just a mouthpiece of the
Junkers, but had attracted to itself other powerful vested
interests alarmed by social disturbance. The party regarded
itself with justice as the most uncompromising opponent of
the November revolution.

The election results have usually been represented as a
victory for the Republic. The Majority Social Democrats,
the Centre Party and the Democrats between them obtained
a solid majority. On the left, the Spartakists boycotted the
election and the Independent Social Democrats only
returned twenty-two deputies out of 423. The DNVP and
Stresemann's DVP combined could only muster 14·7 per
cent of the vote, which gave a total of 63 seats to the anti-
Republican right. Hence monarchism on the one hand and
radical socialism on the other seemed to have been defeated.
Nevertheless, this impression of the election, which was
strengthened by the rapid entry of Democrats and Centre
Party members into a coalition government with the SPD,
is slightly misleading.

The election campaign was fought by the moderate parties as much to protect Germany from socialist dictatorship as to preserve the Republic against reaction. Ever since the outbreak of the revolution their main objective had been to return as quickly as possible to normal forms of parliamentary government. As soon as they had recovered from the first shock of seeing the Empire collapse they, and the majority of the press, began to attack symptoms of anarchy in Germany and to demand law, order and a National Assembly. Many newspapers were almost hysterical in their assaults on the Spartakists, while the Workers' and Soldiers' Councils were seen as rivals to properly elected democratic institutions.

The other major domestic topic to concern the electorate was social policy. The parties recognised that a strong distaste for an unrestricted form of capitalism, with its apparent encouragement of class conflict, existed in Germany at the end of the war. It was almost as though the Germans had come to desire social change as a consolation prize for their military defeat. Both groups of socialists promised socialisation; the Independents with great fervour. Such a policy did not recommend itself to the other parties. They all produced schemes of social reform, diminishing in effectiveness from left to right, but at the same time they stressed their wish to protect private property.

The Democrats presented themselves as being above the class struggle, and ready to defend individual rights.* The Centre Party rejected any attacks on private property. Its speakers were egged on by episcopal pronouncements to the effect that between Christianity and Socialism there could be no compromise – 'only either–or'.[10] The general impression given was that religion and property were threatened,

---

* The banker Hjalmar Schacht, for example, writing in 1926 when revolution was not regarded with favour, claimed that the prime object of those who founded the Democratic Party was to establish internal order in Germany and save the country from Bolshevism.[9]

and that the Centre was a safe refuge from atheist revolution. The two right-wing parties, the DVP and the DNVP, were naturally just as critical of social democracy.

To sum up, the election result of January 1919 was as much a vote against the revolution as for the Republic. The election of the National Assembly sealed the fate of plans for socialisation, the consolidation of the councils system and the fundamental reorganisation of Germany's state authorities. The parliamentary majority which had been eclipsed in November 1918 had now returned. There had never been grounds for great confidence in its ability to function effectively. The events of the revolution had deepened the cleavage between the working-class supporters of the SPD and the nervous liberals or Roman Catholics who had voted for their coalition partners. It was not a good beginning for a government facing immensely difficult tasks.

The National Assembly met in Weimar on 6 February 1919. Weimar lies about one hundred and fifty miles southwest of Berlin, and was chosen as the home of the National Assembly because the capital was not considered safe.

The Assembly's main task was to agree on the form of the new German State and draw up a constitution. Negotiations over this were inevitably long and complicated. Apart from obvious problems which beset all constitution makers – the type of political representation to be chosen, the division of powers within the State, and the nature of the executive – the Germans had to tackle a difficulty which had troubled the founders of their previous Empire: the existence of the German Federal States.

These states, or *Länder* as they are more properly called, pre-dated the Empire. Many of them, like Saxony, Bavaria and Württemberg, had long histories and a strong sense of local patriotism. They were, however, very uneven in size, and their geographical position was not designed to facilitate a federal type of government. By far the largest was the

kingdom of Prussia, which had dominated Germany before
the revolution. It contained 57 per cent of Germany's
population and extended from the Rhine to the Russian
frontier. Under the Imperial constitution the Länder had
been allowed to keep their own governments and their own
parliamentary institutions. Most of the domestic administration in Germany was carried out by officials in the employ
of Land governments. Prussia, whose electoral system had
been weighted in favour of the propertied classes, was
naturally very important in this administrative scheme, and
its government had always been a bulwark of Imperial
authority. It was not surprising that reformers in the
Empire had wanted to see Prussia's dominating position
abolished. Social Democrats and left-wing liberals were in
favour of rationalising Germany's administrative structure
so as to create a stronger central government in Berlin and
smaller, more uniform administrative units for local affairs.[11]
It was, of course, also assumed that both national and local
authorities would be strictly democratic in their election
and methods.

The Minister of the Interior in the new coalition government was a Democrat, Hugo Preuss, who taught Constitutional Law at the Commercial University in Berlin.[12] As
early as 14 November 1918 he had been empowered by
Ebert to draw up plans for a constitution. A firm believer
in drastic reform, he particularly admired the British
system of local government, although his ideas about it
were rather utopian. His ideal conception of a new Germany
would have involved not only a radical reconstruction of
the Länder so as to create units of roughly equal size, but
also a great diminution in their status. They would have
become little more than the provincial element in a
pyramid of democratically elected local authorities.[13] Such
changes were clearly too sweeping to gain acceptance.
Preuss therefore watered down his proposals to a certain
extent, and when he published his draft constitution on

20 January 1919 the Reich was seen to preserve its Federal character. But it was clear that some smaller Länder were likely to be eliminated, Prussia would be broken up and the powers of all the Länder reduced *vis-à-vis* the central government in Berlin.[14]

Preuss's plans had much to commend them in theory, but they soon ran into practical difficulties. At the root of these lay the interest which many party politicians felt in maintaining the old administrative structure. The events of the revolution in various Länder had strengthened particularist feelings there. Whatever theorists might say, the regional organisations of all parties – including the Socialists and the Democrats – had never been wildly keen to see their Länder emasculated. The events of the revolution had strengthened these particularist feelings, because the old opposition parties had been able to take over the reins of government in the Länder capitals as well as in Berlin. In particular, Prussia, once the bastion of Hohenzollern power, now became a stronghold of the Social Democrats, who – usually in alliance with the Centre – maintained an unbroken influence over the Prussian Land government until 1932.

It was also unfortunate for Preuss that his draft should be published at a time when the Reich government itself looked very insecure. Many provincial politicians were afraid that Berlin might fall prey to Bolshevism. There was a widely-voiced fear that the dissolution of Prussia would encourage the French and the Poles to covet parts of her old territory. Hence Preuss's scheme ran into great opposition from the Länder, and Ebert's government felt in no position to ride roughshod over such objections. In any case, some of Ebert's own colleagues felt alarm at the thought of Prussia being weakened.[15]

After a great deal of wrangling a compromise was arrived at whereby the Länder kept their historic form and their administrative institutions. Certain privileges in taxation,

rail and postal services and military affairs which had been
enjoyed by some of the southern states were abolished.
Although some of the powers previously enjoyed by Land
governments were now transferred to that of the Reich, the
execution of Germany's laws was still mainly in the hands
of officials controlled by the Länder. Police, judges and
school teachers were employed by state governments rather
than by the authorities in Berlin. The major exception to
this state of affairs lay in the field of taxation, where
Erzberger – who became Germany's Finance Minister in
June 1919 – insisted on establishing tax-gathering agencies
under the direct control of the central government.[16]
Procedure was established for the future modification of
Land boundaries, but no major changes were ever made.*
The Prussian state remained intact.

Given the difficult situation faced by the Republic in the
early months of 1919 such a compromise arrangement was
not surprising, but it could hardly be described as a happy
solution. On the one hand the constitution was not de-
centralised enough for those who thought that the Länder
should have as much autonomy as was compatible with the
needs of German unity. On the other it did not establish a
single, unrivalled source of power in the Reich.

The fact that Reich laws took priority over Land laws
did not prevent Land governments ignoring orders from
Berlin, or trying to obstruct them. On several occasions in
the career of the Republic the conflict between Land and
Reich authorities was to threaten the stability of the whole
State. It certainly made effective policy-making in Berlin
very difficult. At the same time party politics remained
organised on a Land basis so that regional struggles for
power could, and did, have an effect on relations between

* Thuringia was united as a Land in 1920, and in the same year
Coburg was joined to Bavaria. Pyrmont joined Prussia in 1922. In 1928
there was an exchange of territory between Saxony and Prussia, and
Waldeck joined Prussia. None of these changes was of a radical
character.[17]

the parties in Berlin. In addition the Länder themselves had a voice in the Reich legislature, the second chamber of which, the Reichsrat, was made up of their representatives. Although the major initiative for legislation came from the Reichstag, the Reichsrat could exercise considerable influence over it.[18]

If the relationships between the Reich and the Länder were never satisfactorily resolved, the constitution-makers were more successful with problems of a more conventional kind. The position of the Republic's President, for example, was difficult to define. Should he simply be a constitutional figurehead? Or a democratically elected commander of the executive as in the United States of America? A compromise between these two extremes was chosen. The President was to be elected by popular vote, but the Reich Chancellor (Prime Minister) whom he nominated was responsible to parliament. The President was given the right to govern by decree in the event of a national emergency, so long as his measures were not rejected in parliament. It was clear that excessive reliance on these presidential powers would damage German democracy. The fact that between 1930 and 1932 German governments had to fall back on the authority of President Hindenburg was a grave admission of weakness, but it has never been satisfactorily explained what the alternatives to presidential rule could have been. Certainly the President's powers came in very useful for the defenders of the Republic during other turbulent times; notably the crisis year of 1923. Despite having the authority of popular elections* no President attempted a *coup d'état* along the lines of Louis Napoleon. Hitler established his dictatorship while he was Reich Chancellor.

At the heart of the constitution lay the Reichstag, the national parliament, which was to be elected by universal suffrage under a system of proportional representation.

* Ebert was never popularly elected, so this actually only applies to Hindenburg.

Since such elections would normally only take place every four years an element of direct democracy – the plebiscite – was introduced. Theoretically it was possible for conflicts between the two legislative houses, the Reichstag and the Reichsrat, or between the President and the legislature to be settled by this means. In addition, if 10 per cent of the electorate petitioned for a particular piece of legislation and the Reichstag refused to carry it into law the matter could be put before the whole nation for a plebiscitary decision. These provisions had little practical value. The plebiscite did not recommend itself to administrators as a means of overcoming constitutional difficulties because it might lead to popular unrest. They preferred negotiations behind the scenes. A number of attempts were made by political parties to organise plebiscites in favour of controversial measures, but none of these proposals ever succeeded.[19] Plebiscitary campaigns may have helped to poison the political atmosphere in Germany – the Nationalist assault on the Young Plan in 1929 was an example of this – but they did not play a vital part in the Republic's development.

One other feature of the constitution has come in for particular criticism. This was the system of proportional representation under which members of the Reichstag were to be elected. Proportional representation had long been a political objective of the Social Democrats because, under the old Imperial method of constituency elections in which members were elected by a simple majority, urban voters usually elected fewer members than country voters. Hence the vote of a Bavarian peasant counted for more than that of a factory hand in Berlin. The National Assembly had therefore been elected according to a method invented by a Belgian, de Hondte. The country was divided into thirty-eight large electoral districts, and parties put up lists of candidates in each of these.* The number of votes cast for a

* Elections were actually held in only thirty-seven of the districts, because the French did not allow voting in Alsace-Lorraine.

party in any electoral district decided how many candidates from its list would be sent to the Assembly. This system was continued under the new constitution, but was modified so that for every 60,000 votes a party received it could count one Reichstag member, while its surplus votes in all districts should be pooled to elect extra members from a national party list. In this way virtually no vote was wasted.[20]

It has often been argued that proportional representation weakened Germany by fostering a multiplicity of small parties and thus preventing the emergence of large political forces concerned with national issues. Another unattractive feature of the electoral system was that voters could not select persons when voting, only lists. Hence the position of a candidate on a list was all-important, and this was decided by his party organisation in the region concerned. This seemed to make party officials more important than the electorate in the career of German politicians.

Such criticisms have some weight, but are not convincing explanations of the Republic's political difficulties. So far as the relationship between parties and electorate is concerned, it would be naïve to imagine that single-member constituencies produce a much closer association between a member of parliament and his voters. In Britain, for example, it is clear that most electors vote for the party rather than the man. The party machine is as important in small constituencies as it is in large ones. Nor was the need to please local sentiment absent from the minds of German committee-men. Some members of the Reichstag enjoyed greater popularity with their electors than others, but this is a phenomenon common to all electoral systems.

As for the question of small parties, and the supposed fragmentation of Germany's political life, it should be remembered that all of the major parties in the German National Assembly were direct successors of those represented in the Imperial Reichstag. In one case – the DNVP – the new party was an amalgamation of several old ones and therefore represented consolidation rather than diversification of forces. Other small groups, like the Danes and the Poles, had vanished. Smaller parties did become more successful electorally towards the end of the 1920s – and the liberal middle class was particularly affected by this development – but all the small groups put together never attracted more than 15 per cent of the total vote in German elections. It is also doubtful how far the proportional system helped those parties dedicated to the destruction of the Republic. The Nazis and the Communists were parties whose main strength lay outside parliament, but it is unlikely that any other electoral method would have held them back.

So far as Hitler's party was concerned, it may have benefited somewhat from proportional representation in the election of 1930, when it first became a serious parliamentary threat to the established parties. But by 1932 it had increased its support so much that under an electoral system such as that used in Britain it would actually have gained an absolute majority over all the other parties. Hitler was never able to win such a majority, even in the highly pressurised election of March 1933, whereas without proportional representation he would then have been given the two-thirds majority he needed to alter the constitution. In that case the Nazi claim to have achieved absolute power as the result of democratic processes would have seemed unanswerable.[21]

Whatever problems faced the Weimar Republic they were not attributable to the democratic nature of its constitution. Far more important was the legacy of the old Wilhelmine Empire, in which parliamentary parties had been given rights of self-expression without being required to shoulder the duties of government. In the Weimar Republic these parties retained the lack of responsibility which had characterised their behaviour in the old Reichstag. This did not mean that their leaders were unpatriotic or deliberately feckless. But by tradition politicians who participated in coalition governments remained bound by the decisions of their own party delegation, and the delegation in its turn was mightily influenced by pressures from party organisations outside parliament. The result was that fruitful collaboration between party leaders in cabinet might be torpedoed by a party committee fearful of associating itself with electorally unpopular measures or persons. For this, as for the structural inadequacies of the German State, the Republic was less to be blamed than its Imperial predecessor.

The Republic's first parliamentary cabinet took office in February 1919. It was a coalition of Majority Socialists, Democrats and Centre. An alliance of moderate working-class social democracy, middle-class liberalism and organised Roman Catholicism, it came to be known as the Weimar Coalition. Such a combination aroused fury in the breasts of many who had been associated with the old Reich, for it seemed that the least patriotic elements had seized the reins of power and were feathering their own nests at Germany's expense. It was especially galling for them to see the Catholics, whom they had unjustly supposed were more loyal to Rome than Berlin, working hand in glove with irreligious Social Democrats. These negative views were widespread among sections of German society whose power and influence had by no means disappeared. The army, and later on the powerful ex-servicemen's association, the *Stahlhelm*, were especially prone to resentments of this kind. They were also to be encountered in the universities and among civil servants.

As for the coalition itself, co-operation was genuine among the leaders of the government parties in the National Assembly, but their motives were mixed and the attitude of their supporters unenthusiastic. The Democrats and Centre joined the government primarily to prevent the Social Democrats exercising a monopoly of power. The Centre

Party, in particular, had serious doubts about committing itself to the new administration. Many of its rank and file upbraided the leadership for betraying the anti-socialist pledges made at the elections.[22]

The coalition was soon faced with great internal stress as the result of the Allied peace terms to Germany, presented on 1 May. Reluctance to shoulder responsibility for accepting a harsh peace caused ministers to resign, and the Democrats withdrew from the coalition for several months. Internal strife also discredited the government.

As Germany's constitution-makers debated in the National Theatre at Weimar, rumblings of proletarian disturbance provided a sinister chorus in the wings. In the spring of 1919, the Russian Bolshevik goal of world revolution seemed nearer than at any other time. That January the Soviet government, whose communications with the West were uneven and eccentric, established a new international socialist organisation – the Comintern. In March a Communist *coup* took place in Hungary, where Bela Kun set up a dictatorship in Budapest. German Austria appeared to be on the brink of revolution. There were strikes in the Ruhr and disturbances in Berlin. Most spectacular of all were the events in Bavaria. In February Kurt Eisner, having been overwhelmingly defeated at elections for a new Bavarian parliament, was on his way to announce his resignation when an unsophisticated young aristocrat shot him dead.

In the wave of popular indignation which followed, the Workers' and Soldiers' Councils became the real source of authority in Munich. On 7 April a group of radicals declared Bavaria to be a Soviet Republic. A week later leadership of the Soviet was taken over by the Communist Party, at whose head stood a dedicated young Russian revolutionary, Eugen Leviné. A Red Army was recruited. Lenin sent his blessing to the Bavarians. It was not until 1 May 1919 that Noske's troops from northern Germany and some Bavarian Freikorps fought their way into Munich. The Soviet was crushed with much brutality. Many revolutionaries were shot without trial, and others received terms of imprisonment. Leviné himself, having courageously defended his beliefs before a special court, was condemned to death and executed.

The Munich Soviet was by no means the only instance of revolutionary unrest in 1919. The spectacle of Reichswehr units, often still in the form of Freikorps, marching into German cities to suppress working-class unrest became almost commonplace. Although the Communists afterwards claimed that they had borne the brunt of such fighting, their organisation was feeble and their numbers insignificant. The Independent Social Democratic Party was still the spokesman – albeit a confused and divided spokesman – of the radical proletariat.

Yet the USPD never really adjusted itself to the post-war situation. It wanted both social revolution and democracy, and however desirable these objectives may have been, they were not compatible in the Germany of 1919. Many of the more distinguished members of the party had always rejected the concept of a Soviet dictatorship. Although they were bitter about the way their former comrades in the SPD had treated them they were basically men of peace and compromise. For them the road back into the old Social Democratic Party was easier to tread than that which led to Bolshevik revolution.

At first, no such choice had to be made. The USPD, whose leaders were not burdened with government responsibility and whose speakers defended rebellious elements in parliament and the law courts, reaped a handsome reward in working-class gratitude. At the Republic's first Reichstag elections of June 1920 the party quadrupled its representation and more than doubled its vote. It was a hollow victory. Virtually isolated on the left, the Independents could do little in parliament and were divided on the extent to which they should carry the battle out into the streets. An immediate cause of dissension faced the party in the autumn of 1920 when it was suggested that the Independents should submit themselves to the discipline of the Third (Communist) International, directed from Moscow. A majority of the delegates at a Party Congress in October accepted this move, but in practice only about a third of the party's membership actually left to join the Communists.[23] Nevertheless, this was the beginning of the end for the Independents, and in 1922 the rump of the party voted to rejoin the Majority Social Democrats.

Hence, for all its weakness, the Communist Party possessed certain long-term advantages in the battle for the allegiance of the left. Its revolutionary martyrs – Liebknecht, Rosa Luxemburg, and even Leviné – achieved wider notoriety than their equivalents in the USPD, largely because the most prominent figures in that party did not figure in revolutionary upheavals. The party also gained from the sinister prestige of its Bolshevik patrons in Soviet Russia. It was natural that the Government should place most of the blame for violence on the 'Reds' or Communists, thus adding to the impression that the KPD was the only effective champion of proletarian dictatorship in Germany.

Unrest on the left forced the Republican government to rely more heavily on the repressive authorities associated with the old Empire. First among these was the army, now renamed the *Reichswehr* and under the direction of staff officers whose emotional loyalties were almost entirely directed towards the old Reich of Bismarck. By the summer of 1919 they were beginning to recover their confidence after the shocks of the revolutionary period.

The new Reichswehr was the first unified army Germany had possessed in peacetime. Its headquarters were those of the former Prussian War Ministry in Berlin's Bendlerstrasse. The army was built up out of the loyal remnants of old units and some of the new Freikorps, although staff officers were not too enthusiastic about the self-willed attitude apparent in these formations. The official aim was to develop a consolidated and highly disciplined force, completely dependent on the orders of its military superiors. The question of obedience was supremely important; the existence of Soldiers' Councils had apparently threatened the internal cohesion of the army and undermined the status of the officers.

In fact the officer corps was fighting a very successful battle not only to survive, but also to maintain its exclusive control over the armed services. Bloodshed and disorder in various parts of the country in the first half of 1919 made the new Reichswehr indispensable to the government. Gustav Noske, the minister responsible, brooked no interference with the troops on ideological grounds. He was confident that he could work with the generals of the old army and obtain their loyal co-operation.

In any case, there seemed no alternative. Few socialists and trade unionists felt much enthusiasm for the army. Noske's appeals for co-operation in recruiting fell on stony ground within his own party. There were many reasons for this. The socialists had always been hostile to the military even though many of them – including Noske – had admitted before 1914 that there was a need for national defence. The behaviour of the military towards proletarian insurgents disgusted many trade unionists and alienated the socialist press. Apart from these political problems there was an institutional difficulty which became important after the peace treaty was signed. The Allies insisted that the new German army should not be based on conscription, but should consist of long-service professional soldiers. Very few urban workers desired to sign on for twelve years in a force whose political and social characteristics they found unattractive. The officer corps was able to recruit men to its own taste – indeed it had little choice. Most Reichswehr recruits were from rural areas, and few had Social-

Democratic, or even specifically Republican sympathies. Hence the spirit of the old army survived. The Soldiers' Councils dwindled in importance until they were eliminated. Noske, energetic though he was, could not prevent the staff officers – of whom a disproportionately large number had been kept in service as the army was demobilised – from keeping the control of military affairs very much in their own hands. As the political position of the Republican coalition became weaker so the independence of the men in the Bendlerstrasse grew more marked.

In the civil service the story was often similar, although always more complicated. When the revolution broke out most of the former officials in Reich and Land administrations had been asked to stay at their posts. Even the Workers' and Soldiers' Councils had reluctantly realised that to dispense with them was impossible. They had attempted to place the bureaucracy under proletarian supervision, but such efforts were never successful.

Although the more ambitious plans of the Workers' and Soldiers' Councils to supplant or subordinate the bureaucracy came to nothing, it was clear that the new Republican coalition would wish to exert an influence over the recruitment and personnel of the civil service. It was also hoped that the power of officialdom would be diminished and that parliament would exercise greater control over civil servants than had been possible under the old régime.

No such developments took place. The civil service remained a powerful force at all levels of society. Its numbers swelled after 1919. The revolution did not damage the authority and status of the official; on the contrary, his position was strengthened. Under the new Constitution he could not be dismissed on political grounds, yet he was given the right to participate in political life, and could be elected to parliament. In 1930 civil servants were to be found representing all shades of opinion in the Reichstag, nine of them in the Nazi Party.[24]

By no means all officials were hostile to the Republic, but many of them had been shocked by the violence and confusion of the November revolution. They then found themselves working for political parties which had usually been regarded by the official classes under the Empire as subversive or disloyal. This was especially true of the Social Democrats and the Centre. Although officials who served Wilhelm II had liked to regard themselves as above politics, those connected with law enforcement and local government had been expected to exert their influence in favour of 'loyal' parties at election time, and they had usually done so.[25]

There was also the question of professional competence. German administrative officials regarded themselves as models of incorruptible efficiency, and this assessment was not unduly flattering. It was certainly accepted by most of the German middle classes. The training for a senior civil servant was lengthy and nearly always involved legal studies. Hence senior officials were not simply products of a particular class – although most of them came from socially superior backgrounds and the nobility was strongly represented[26] – but regarded themselves as part of a specialised élite. If the Republican parties were going to promote their own candidates into politically sensitive posts they would command respect from existing officials only if they possessed the right qualifications.

For the Centre Party and the Democrats this did not present too serious a problem, since lawyers and members of the judiciary were prominent in their ranks.[27] But the SPD had fewer men with the required background. Its leaders had worked their way up through trade unions, their party's administration or the party press. When such men were appointed to administrative or diplomatic posts it could be suggested that the standards of the service were being lowered for the benefit of party hacks. In actual fact some of the new officials performed very creditably. In the diplomatic service, for example, several ambassadorships were given to men whose careers had been made in the Labour movement, and they performed their tasks with distinction.[28]

The most important administrative area in which considerable changes were made was the state of Prussia. There the Ministry of the Interior was almost continuously under the control of the Social Democrats. The other coalition parties were also in a good position to press for appointments although political support alone was rarely enough to secure an official post. Between 1919 and 1929 there were numerous changes in the Prussian civil service, especially in those sectors of the administration concerned with law enforcement. Many of the new appointees from the Social Democratic side had trade union experience, and this often proved an asset in dealing with labour problems. Although party political patronage was regarded as corrupt by nationalist opponents of the régime, many of those who took up government posts in Prussia lost money by doing so.[29] This was especially true of the early 1920s when, owing to inflation, an official's salary was losing its value all the time.

The charge that the Republic had brought corruption and chaos became commonplace among its monarchist and nationalist opponents, and many bureaucrats believed it to be true. It was significant that a lot of them interpreted their oath to obey the constitution as not implying a commitment to the Republican state form.[30] When Hitler campaigned to 'cleanse' the administration of corrupt Republican elements he was echoing views expressed widely in far more respectable conservative circles.

One particular section of the bureaucracy exercised a definitely negative effect on the Republic's fortunes from the outset. This was the judiciary. The first reason was personal; most of the judges had been appointed by Imperial authorities before the November revolution. The second was legal. Jurists, being concerned with the law, naturally regarded revolution and the arbitrary acts of revolutionary bodies with distaste. The moderate Republicans were, for their part, hampered by the belief that judges ought to be irremovable in order to safeguard fair implementation of the law. Despite various proposals put forward in the Workers' and Soldiers' Councils, there was no such thing as 'revolutionary justice' in Germany.

On the contrary, German jurists glossed over the revolution; they assumed that the Republican government had inherited state authority of the old Reich through a kind of apostolic succession passing from Prince Max of Baden to Friedrich Ebert. Cases of a political nature were judged according to standards which had changed little since the time of Bismarck. It was an unhappy chance that the first political cases to come before the courts in Republican Germany involved conflict between the Republican authorities and their enemies on the left.

It was natural for jurists brought up in an authoritarian tradition to take a harsh view of militant revolutionaries and to condone excesses against them by the forces of law and order. The State Prosecutor in Munich, who later became Bavaria's Minister of Justice and a member of Hitler's cabinet, told one young socialist lawyer that the fighting in Munich in May 1919 should be regarded in the same light as a storm or similar natural disaster; there was no need to pursue the question of Freikorps atrocities too zealously.[31]

This sophistry in the administration of political justice, coinciding as it did with the personal prejudices of many judges, was soon to have more sinister implications. When attacks on the Republic began to come from the right rather than the left the law courts ceased to act as an effective shield. Attempted counter-revolution, political murder and libellous publications were often connived at in the courts because the judges thought the perpetrators more 'patriotic' than the new régime they were attacking.

Many judges were willing to abide by the letter of the Constitution, but they thought that above the Republic – which was the child of party politics – there stood a greater interest, that of the nation. This view, which was also common among other officials and army officers, implied that if Republican politics and what the judiciary considered to be the national interest came into conflict, the former might be cast aside. Since right-wing organisations were usually regarded as 'nationally-minded' this distinction worked to their advantage.

The inability of the new Republic to win the hearts of its servants was symbolised by their reluctance to accept the outward trappings of the new régime. During the early 1920s many civil servants in Prussia happened to take their holidays on the anniversary of the Republican constitution, a day on which they would otherwise have been expected to demonstrate their loyalty to the new state form. The Republican flag, with its black, red and gold colours, was often not flown over public buildings. The army always avoided flying it wherever possible, and succeeded in being granted a special war flag in the old Imperial colours with those of the Republic tucked away ignominiously in one corner.

The outlook for the Republic might have been rosier if a favourable climate of opinion had existed outside official circles. The Third French Republic had survived despite a largely monarchist officer corps and a parliament in which a majority hoped for a monarchist restoration. But after the signature of the Versailles Peace Treaty hopes of progress within the Republic tended to evaporate. In the universities and grammar schools bourgeois youth regarded the new democracy with contempt. Sixth-formers at one school who used the Weimar Constitution for air-gun practice were not untypical of their class and generation. German universities, despite grandiose projects for reform aired during the revolutionary period, remained predominantly a middle-class preserve, where the shame of Versailles was felt especially deeply. As was perhaps not unnatural, Western political ideas became unfashionable among intellectual youth and the search for a German solution to social and political problems led some to Russian Communism, some to authoritarian nationalism and some to a mixture of both. This is not to suggest that there were no young people of liberal or social-democratic persuasion at universities. But the atmosphere in these institutions was not conducive to the development of a stable democracy.

The churches, too, looked back to the old order with nostalgia. In practice they were treated very generously by the Republic. Despite socialist demands for a division of Church and State, neither the religious nor the financial status of the churches was damaged. But the Protestant Church resented losing the national status it had enjoyed under the Empire. Most of its clergy remained openly monarchist. The Roman Catholic Church, for its part, was not so much impressed by the success of the Centre Party as by the threat to property and religion posed by an atheistical revolutionary movement.

It was therefore quite clear that the Republican parties faced an uphill task in associating the German people with their new state. The picture was not entirely black. The trade unions, for example, were committed to the Republic. Between 1914 and 1919 the socialist trade unions increased in membership from two to five-and-a-half millions. By 1920 this figure rose to nearly eight millions, although it dropped away from the peak in the years that followed. The trade unions provided the backbone of the SPD's support electorally, they were a powerful source of financial aid and their newspapers had a readership of some six millions.[32]

Yet the unions had their disadvantages as allies. They were mainly concerned with an economic struggle against capitalism, and although their leaders were usually moderate men they spoke the language of the class war.

This was in any case a characteristic of the whole working-class movement and helped to alienate the Social Democrats' colleagues in the Weimar Coalition. The economic power of the unions was a possible weapon in the socialist armoury, though labour leaders had always been very chary of using it. Its one apparent success came in the Kapp Putsch, but the value of a political strike was soon demonstrated to be very doubtful to a government dependent on middle-class votes. Social Democracy could not hope to wield effective power while the working-class movement remained divided. The other organs of proletarian self-expression which might have aided their cause, the Workers' Councils, had been rapidly emasculated.[33]

Founded on a discredited revolution and burdened with a detested peace treaty, the Republic faced a grim future.

[1] Robson, *Left-Wing Liberalism*, pp. 424–6.

[2] For details of this conflict between Stresemann and those eager to amalgamate the National Liberals with the DDP see Turner, *Stresemann*, pp. 13–25.

[3] Robson, *Left-Wing Liberalism*, pp. 401, 407.

[4] Turner, *Stresemann*, pp. 30, 35.

[5] Robson, *Left-Wing Liberalism*, pp. 372–3, citing Matthias–Morsey, *Prinz Max von Baden*, pp. 631–3.

[6] See Morsey, *Zentrumspartei*, pp. 79 ff., 110–17.

[7] For details of the founding of the DNVP see Hertzmann, *DNVP*, pp. 32 ff.

[8] *Deutsche Nationalversammlung*, vol. I, p. 185. In 1912 the Old Conservatives had been the strongest right-wing party in Posen, Pomerania and East Prussia. The Free Conservatives were stronger in West Prussia.

[9] Schacht, *Stabilization of the Mark*, pp. 36–7. He adheres to the same view in *My First Seventy-Six Years*, pp. 148–52.

[10] Morsey, *Zentrumspartei*, p. 134.

[11] On the attitudes of SPD and Democrats to the Constitution see Schulz, *Demokratie und Diktatur*, vol. I, pp. 30–1, 101 ff.

[12] Eyck, *History*, vol. I, p. 54.

[13] Cf. Schulz, *Demokratie und Diktatur*, pp. 127–30.

[14] For a discussion of the draft see Apelt, *Weimarer Verfassung*, pp. 56–64.

[15] Schulz, *Demokratie und Diktatur*, pp. 136–8.

[16] For Erzberger's part in framing the new taxation system see Epstein, *Matthias Erzberger*, pp. 334–8.

[17] Apelt, *Weimarer Verfassung*, pp. 137–8.

[18] It could, for example, block legislation which did not command a two-thirds majority in the Reichstag. Ibid. p. 245.

[19] One reason was that such a plebiscite needed the participation of a majority of the electorate if a positive result was to be valid. Hence if all those opposing the proposal abstained their votes would be added to those of the genuine abstainers, and only if there was a positive majority of all electors for the measure would it succeed in becoming law. Apelt, *Weimarer Verfassung*, pp. 249–50.

[20] Apelt, *Weimarer Verfassung*, pp. 179–80. This is a somewhat simplified account of the actual procedure.

[21] See Bracher, *Demokratie und Diktatur*, pp. 53–4.

[22] Morsey, *Zentrumspartei*, pp. 169, 172.

[23] Prager, *Geschichte der USPD*, pp. 222–9. Also Angress, *Stillborn Revolution*, pp. 71–2.

[24] Bracher, *Auflösung*, p. 178.

[25] Runge, *Politik und Beamtentum*, p. 21.

[26] Ibid. pp. 169–71.

[27] Ibid. pp. 45–7. Also Morsey, *Zentrumspartei*, pp. 50–2, 155–6.

[28] Holborn in *The Diplomats* (eds. Craig–Gilbert), p. 152.

[29] Runge, *Politik und Beamtentum*, pp. 52–7.

[30] Ibid. pp. 42, 230–1.

[31] Hoegner, *Aussenseiter*, p. 15.

[32] Hunt, *German Social Democracy*, p. 168.

[33] By 1920 there remained only the factory councils, and under a law passed in January of that year their powers were virtually restricted to the representation of employees' interests within a particular works or factory. See Oertzen, *Betriebsräte*, pp. 155–69.

C

4 The Republic makes Peace

IF Germany's domestic situation was bad her international prospects were catastrophic. The revolution had broken out because the German people wanted peace. However well the new government carried out its tasks at home, the failure of peace negotiations would signal its collapse.

The November revolution did not bring about any fundamental changes in German foreign policy. Although Haase, the leader of the Independent Social Democrats, was responsible for foreign affairs, the personnel and attitudes of the German Foreign Ministry remained much as they had been under the Empire. Critical voices were to be heard demanding truly revolutionary developments in German diplomacy, but they were not heeded.

Some left-wing Independents and Spartakists wanted Germany to forge an alliance with the Bolshevik government in Russia. Proletarian solidarity should be the basis of German security. Such a policy was never taken seriously by the Republican leaders. It would have been anathema to Ebert, and Haase himself warned the cabinet that German overtures towards the Bolsheviks might provoke Allied invasion.[1] The Republic did not establish diplomatic relations with Russia. Another radical demand was that Germany should disassociate herself completely from the discredited policies of the Imperial Government. To do this Haase should purge the administration and diplomatic corps of all those compromised by annexationist tendencies during the war. He should admit that Wilhelm II's ministers had been guilty of aggression in 1914. Kurt Eisner, the Independent Social Democratic Premier in Bavaria, was the most forceful advocate of this course. He believed that by demonstrating her reformed character Germany would win the respect of the Western Powers. He went so far as to publish documents from the Bavarian archives demonstrating German complicity in Austrian aggression against Serbia at the outbreak of war. This gesture did nothing to alter the attitude of Germany's enemies, but it aroused understandable fury in Berlin, where Eisner was regarded as a traitor.

Nevertheless, the desire to win approval from the victors influenced the behaviour of Ebert's government. Peace negotiations begun by Prince Max of Baden in October 1918 had referred to President Wilson's famous Fourteen Points. These envisaged a peace of understanding based on national self-determination and international co-operation. Although no mention of the Fourteen Points was made in the armistice signed on 11 November, the Germans always claimed that any peace settlement ought to comply with them.

Since it was clear that Germany, defeated and helpless as she was, could hardly expect benevolence from the French or the British, her new leaders pinned what hopes they had on the Americans. Ebert and the Foreign Ministry wanted to present President Wilson with a picture of Germany as a stable, democratic country, eager to play her part in the World community. In December a new Foreign Minister was appointed. This was the former ambassador to Copenhagen, Count Brockdorff-Rantzau. He was at pains to stress German enthusiasm for the idea of the League of Nations, and declared that Germany would work for the victory of democracy throughout the World. He called for an end to secret diplomatic intrigues, such as those which had encompassed the Great War.

Although the Count had himself been critical of the Imperial government's policies during the war, much of his enthusiasm for a new international order was assumed for the benefit of the victor powers. The Army, the Foreign

Office and the Government all thought that the 'democratic' card was the one to play. It was not very effective. On 4 February 1919, for example, an American officer on a fact-finding mission to Berlin wrote a report which included the words:

Of Brockdorff-Rantzau and the Foreign Office, I was impressed that no change had occurred and that no democratic spirit exists except as circumstances dictate for the moment. No realization as to the changed conditions in the World and in Germany's position in it are in evidence.[2]

The last sentence certainly applied to the man in the street.

The German public was in no way prepared for a harsh peace. The Germans had always been told that the Reich was waging a defensive war, and did not therefore regard themselves as responsible for the disaster which had befallen Europe. In any case, the Imperial government and the Kaiser were gone, and so the man in the street felt free from all liability for Imperial policies. As Ebert himself put it in his speech at the opening of the new German National Assembly in Weimar on 7 February 1919:

Wherefore, by their own testimony, have our enemies fought? To destroy Kaiserism. That has now passed forever; the very fact of this assembly is proof of that. They fought to destroy 'Militarism'; it has been overthrown and lies in pieces never to rise again. According to their solemn proclamations our enemies have been fighting for justice, freedom and a lasting peace.[3]

Ebert himself was well aware that the Allies were unlikely to offer Germany a peace which would please his fellow-countrymen. The Germans had their own conception of what a just settlement should be. They expected to have to surrender Alsace-Lorraine to France and some limited amount of territory to the Poles. But in return they demanded that the German-speaking parts of the old Habsburg Empire should be allowed to join the Reich. On

12 November the Austrian parliament declared German Austria to be part of the German Republic. Ebert later assured the German National Assembly that negotiations would soon begin with Vienna to make Germany 'a nation of brothers'. Gustav Stresemann, formerly one of the most distinguished leaders of the National Liberal Party in the Reichstag, was prepared to give up his opposition to the Republic if union with Austria could be achieved.[4]

The Germans expected to be made full members of Wilson's League of Nations and to be given equality with other powers in the post-war world. They denied that the Allies had any right to impose an indemnity on Germany, although it was clear to them from the Fourteen Points that payment would have to be made for the restoration of devastated areas in Allied countries. On the whole the Germans' vision of the peace would have left their country rather more powerful *vis-à-vis* its European neighbours than when it entered the war.

It was not likely that the Allies would tolerate such a development. Their peace-makers were, indeed, faced with unique problems, and it took them many months to hammer out their proposals. The previous balance of power in Europe had been totally destroyed. Russia was in a state of civil war and her government seemed quite unfitted to form part of a European concert. The Habsburg Empire was in dissolution and the Ottoman Empire had ceased to exist. France and Belgium suffered directly as the result of war and occupation. Britain had sustained severe financial and human losses. Italy ended the war in a state of collapse. The United States had supported the Western war effort with loans even before it became involved in the fighting. Despite a genuine belief in the need for a new approach to international affairs, the Allies could not be expected to sacrifice their own interests in Germany's favour.

In particular, the victors had to find some means of giving permanent security to France. As Lord Balfour somewhat unkindly put it: 'The Franco-German problem appears insoluble for it is really a problem of making one Frenchman go as far as two Germans.'[5]

Although the British and the Americans offered guarantees to the French, many of them, including Marshal Foch the commander-in-chief, would have preferred more tangible forms of security. They thought in terms of establishing France's frontier on the Rhine and dismembering the German Reich by giving independence to some German areas in the south and west. Such hopes were not realised in the peace settlement but they did not die for several years.

On the question of indemnity the Allied Powers could point to the fact that German industry had been undamaged by occupation in the war. If treated as an equal with the victors Germany's powerful economy might soon dominate Europe.

The Allies presented their peace terms to the Germans on 1 May 1919. They were far more severe than anything the German public had been led to expect. From that time on Germany's foreign policy was systematically directed towards their revision. All parties denounced the Allied proposals and the government averred that it would never accept them.

Summed up very briefly the German case was as follows. First there had been no negotiated settlement, but a *Diktat* forced on Germany by threat of occupation. The Germans had not been able to put their case as equal participants in a peace conference. Although they had presented detailed written objections to the Treaty, they had only been able to obtain a few alterations, and there the bargaining virtually ceased. The Allies attached a time limit to their revised draft. Refusal to agree would mean military invasion.

Secondly, it was argued that the terms imposed on Germany were incompatible with the Wilsonian Fourteen Points, even as revised by Wilson in the light of British and French objections. Germany lost 13 per cent of her territory and about six million subjects. She received nothing in return; Austria was not allowed to join the German Reich. The Germans bitterly resented the territorial settlement on their eastern frontier, where German minorities would be ruled by Poles. In order to give Poland an outlet to the sea the province of East Prussia was cut off from the Reich by a strip of territory joining Poland to the Baltic. This was the famous 'Polish Corridor'. The population of the corridor was, in fact, predominantly Polish, but the port which stood at its head, Danzig, was German. Originally the Allies had intended to give Danzig to the Poles, but on the insistence of Lloyd George it was established as a Free City with an independent administration watched over by a Commissioner for the League of Nations. Further to the east the German city of Memel was ceded to Lithuania. Another eastern area over which there was fierce argument was Upper Silesia, whose population was mixed, but with an overall majority of Germans. After German protests at the Allied proposal to hand this province over to Poland it was agreed that a plebiscite should be organised there. Otherwise the Germans lost Alsace-Lorraine to France, frontier districts to Belgium and Denmark, and the important coal-mining region of the Saar Basin, which was placed under virtual French control for a minimum of fifteen years. This last measure was completely without justification so far as national self-determination was concerned, but was designed to guarantee compensation to the French for the damage done to their industry during the war.

Germany also lost all her colonies, which were distributed to the victors under the overall authority of the League of Nations. The League's involvement seemed a mere fig-leaf to the Germans. For one thing, they themselves were refused entry into the League; for another they did not believe that their enemies would permit colonial policy to be affected by an international body. In this German suspicions were completely justified.

Internationally Germany was not given equality of status

with the victor powers. Brockdorff-Rantzau had already warned the Allies against treating Germany like a ship kept in quarantine as a plague risk.[6] But that was exactly what happened. Germany would only be allowed membership of the League of Nations when she had proved her peaceable character. This strengthened the already widespread feeling in Germany that the League would just be an Association of Victors designed to maintain the supremacy of the Entente Powers. Germany had to submit to disarmament without receiving guarantees that her enemies would disarm also. The German army was to be cut to 100,000 men, and deprived of offensive weapons. The air force was destroyed, the navy reduced to insignificance. In the economic sphere Germany had to accord most-favoured-nation treatment to her enemies but had no such rights herself. A further humiliation was the fact that Allied troops were to remain in occupation of parts of the Rhineland for at least fifteen years as a guarantee that the terms of the treaty would be honoured, and that even after their withdrawal Germany should refrain from fortifying the left bank of the Rhine.

So far as economic and financial issues were concerned, the Germans lost overseas investments confiscated by the Allies. They lost most of their mercantile marine. They had to agree to pay reparations for damage done to Allied civilians during the war, and it became clear that this damage was to be interpreted in a very generous way, even including pensions paid to wounded servicemen and their families.

The Allies established commissions to supervise reparations and the disarmament clauses, so that the Germans could feel that their country was being controlled and exploited by her enemies. It was common to claim that the Allies were determined to extort the last drop of sweat from German workers for the benefit of Western capitalists. There is no doubt that the reparations clauses in the treaty were among the least felicitous elements in the peace settlement. Whatever the justice of Allied claims, the manner in which they were presented was bound to cause trouble in the future. Nobody could expect the Germans to work as well for foreigners as they would for themselves. If the Allies were determined to extort large sums from Germany over a long period they should have been prepared to do so by force. Only the French and the Belgians were ready to face this consequence.

It is certainly true that German criticisms of the treaty were exaggerated. In many cases there were good reasons why conditions which the Germans described as unacceptable should have been imposed on them. Austria was the most obvious example. The Allies could hardly allow Germany to end the war more powerful than she began it, and this would have been the case if a Greater Germany had been created. So far as the Polish Corridor and Danzig were concerned, the Poles had been promised access to the sea in Wilson's Fourteen Points. The settlement of nationality problems involved less injustice than had the frontiers of 1914, when French, Danish and Polish minorities had been included in Germany. The erection of tariff barriers against German goods and the economic burdens on Germany had to be set against the destruction of industrial areas in northern France and Belgium and the losses sustained by Allied merchant fleets as the result of U-boat warfare.

But much more important than the fairness or unfairness of the treaty was its impact on the new German Republic. How far is it true that the Versailles Treaty wrecked German democracy? That Germany's economy was ruined by reparations and her security was undermined by the restrictions on her army? That her status as a European Power was incompatible with the conditions she had to accept? Economically and demographically speaking there was no foundation in these assertions. German industry, despite the losses incurred, soon began to recover its productive capacity. There was a set-back in 1923, but by 1927 the Gross National Product of the Weimar Republic had exceeded that of the entire German Reich in 1913. Germany's population was still half as large again as that of France and continued to rise. If the aim of French statesmen had been, as one English critic averred, to 'set the clock back and to undo what, since 1870, the progress of Germany had accomplished'[7] it had not been successful.

Germany's currency certainly suffered a complete disaster in the years following the peace treaty, and many outside experts, as well as virtually all Germans, blamed this on the reparations burden.[8] But there were other factors involved. Germany's internal debt had been greatly increased during the war, and of course she received no reparations to meet that. The Republican governments of the period also seemed incapable of imposing stringent fiscal measures on tax-payers and banks. This was directly related to the peace settlement, since it was believed that more effective government control would simply mean that more of Germany's wealth would drain away to the Allies.

From the economic point of view the Versailles Treaty offered very little hope of settling Europe's problems. It was possible to imagine, however, that as time passed the international organisation which had been established as part of the peace settlement might create improvements. Positive collaboration between victors and vanquished would be needed if the economic difficulties created by the war were to be overcome.

Much more serious was the political demoralisation which the treaty caused within the Reich itself. This was not so important among those already inclined to attack the Republic as among the democratic parties which supported it. The Nationalists and the Communists had already made it clear before June 1919 that they would not be contented with the new state form. Hitler would have raved against

Versailles whatever its terms had been. The real damage the treaty did to Germany was to disillusion more moderate men who might otherwise have supported their new Republic. The parties most seriously harmed as a result were those which formed the Republican coalition, the Social Democrats, the Democrats, and the Centre Party. These groups were forced to turn to the German people after an apparently successful revolution with nothing to offer them but failure. The political gains of that revolution actually had been considerable, but to the public mind they remained unimpressive. The Germans had a new constitution; to many of them the old one had seemed good enough. They had more freedom politically but most of them had thought of themselves as free before. They had responsible government; this 'responsibility' seemed to mean confusion and even bloodshed in home affairs. The one thing that the new order had brought them – peace – had been transformed by a settlement which their newspapers and political leaders all agreed was a form of prolonged slavery for Germany. It was not an encouraging start.

Two particular issues connected with the peace settlement continued to poison the political atmosphere in Germany for many years. The first was the question of war guilt. It had seemed self-evident to the victor powers that the Germans had committed aggression in 1914. Article 231 of the peace treaty required them to accept responsibility for the war as the legal basis for Allied reparations claims against Germany. The Germans vigorously rejected this and demanded an impartial enquiry into the origins of the war. By treating the matter as one of central importance the Germans provoked the Allied governments to reiterate their view that Germany had been the aggressor. This made compromise more difficult.[9]

After the treaty was signed the German Foreign Office did not relax its efforts to prove to the world that the Germans did not start the Great War. Historians were mobilised to sift through Germany's diplomatic documents and demonstrate that Imperial policies – though sometimes misguided – were not basically warlike. Every opportunity was taken to publicise expert opinion which seemed to support Germany's case. Academics in foreign countries – especially among neutral states and in the U.S.A. – were canvassed for interpretations of war guilt favourable to Germany.* In the two decades after the war a school of 'revisionist' historians appeared conducting an academic argument which had direct political implications. The world of scholarship doubtless benefited from the diplomatic documents which became available as a result of this argument. But during the Weimar Republic the consequences were not happy for Germany. By attacking the whole foundation of the Allied peace plan the Germans aroused the suspicion that they did not really intend to abide by it. At home it was believed that Germany could never be prosperous or safe so long as she was still 'shackled' by an unjust peace settlement. Diplomatically speaking it was not until Hitler came to power that the effects of the German campaign against 'war guilt' came to be felt. Then it was the Nazis who reaped the benefit of the industrious efforts by academics, journalists and diplomats to undermine the moral basis of the European peace settlement.

The second issue was that of the so-called 'stab-in-the-back'. Attempts to deny war guilt had domestic implications. If Germany had not been responsible for the war – as even Republican ministers claimed – then the Imperial authorities could not be blamed for the catastrophe which had befallen their country. Indeed, from the moral viewpoint, Germany in no way deserved to be defeated in the war. How could this military injustice have come about?

* The German Foreign Office set up a special subsection, the *Kriegsschuldreferat*, to inspire and subsidise a campaign proving the Germans innocent of responsibility for the war.[10] This is not to suggest that the historians in Germany and elsewhere who supported this campaign did not sincerely believe that their case was just.

Was it not true that Germany had been on the brink of victory in the early summer of 1918? How could she possibly have won so many battles, gained so much enemy territory and still have been defeated?

For those who had pressed for ambitious annexations and total victory the answer was obvious. It was the fault not of superior Allied force, still less of superior Allied strategy. The real culprits were to be found within the frontiers of Germany. They were the weaklings and backsliders (the *Flaumacher*), the pacifists, socialists and other revolutionaries who had undermined Germany's war effort.

The German army, unbeaten in the field, had been stabbed in the back. The blame for Germany's defeat rested on the politicians at home. This accusation against the founders of Germany's Republic was not the result of disappointed idealism caused by the Treaty of Versailles. It had been current even before the war ended and had grown in strength ever since. Despite attempts to increase its credibility by attributing it to a British general, the 'stab-in-the-back' was a home-grown product.* It became, like the war-guilt theory, a subject of endless discussion and publicity. Newspaper campaigns, libel actions and even a parliamentary committee of enquiry fanned the flames of controversy and reinforced the public impression that some sinister secret underlay Germany's defeat in the war. Republican politicians were once again on the defensive, and their own ambivalence towards the November revolution made it difficult for them to counter-attack.

---

* The aim was to cite foreign opinion in support of a German myth. Actually two British officers – Lieutenant-General Maurice and Major-General Malcolm – were credited with inventing the stab-in-the-back. Maurice's published statements were exaggerated in the German press and Malcolm himself had simply paraphrased a long-winded diatribe by Ludendorff. The idea of the stab-in-the-back pre-dated both British comments. This did not stop Hindenburg referring to 'an English General' as his authority when blaming German defeat on disintegration behind the lines.[11]

The decision to accept the peace treaty was not taken without agonising deliberations. Brockdorff-Rantzau refused to sign it, and the Prime Minister, Scheidemann, resigned. In addition to opposition from the political parties and most of the press, powerful military pressure was exerted on the Government to refuse the Western peace terms. Reinhardt, the Prussian Minister of War and chief of the new German army, feared that signature of the treaty would provoke mutiny among his troops. The proposed restrictions on Germany's armed forces were a direct threat to the careers of all men in uniform. Plans were adumbrated for a last-ditch resistance in the eastern provinces of Germany, it being believed that the Poles could be successfully opposed if they intervened. There were important men in the officer corps urging a military *coup* against the government if it capitulated to the Allies. Hopes for such a stroke were pinned on Field-Marshal Hindenburg, but – not for the first time in his career – the old war hero evaded responsibility for a political decision. It was left to his more energetic colleague, General Groener, to persuade the senior officers who controlled the armed forces that resistance to the treaty would result in the dismemberment of Germany. It was better to keep the German people together under humiliating conditions than to risk their complete disintegration.[12]

The National Assembly was still reluctant to capitulate to the Allies. The energetic intervention of Ebert – now acting President of the Republic – was needed to obtain an affirmative vote to the peace proposals. So great was the feeling of national humiliation that the parties who agreed to accept the Allied terms demanded a statement from their opponents recognising that only patriotic motives had influenced their decision.

On 28 June 1919 the peace treaty was signed in the Hall of Mirrors at Versailles by Hermann Müller, the Social Democratic Foreign Minister, and Dr Hans Bell, a Centre

Party member who was Minister of Transport. The war had thus been formally brought to an end nearly eight months after hostilities had originally been suspended.

Should the treaty have been resisted? Might it not have been healthier if the national revulsion at the treaty had found expression in a physical conflict which would at least have forced the Allies to make themselves directly responsible for the imposition of their own peace terms? Would not even an enemy occupation have been preferable to a peace which burdened Germany's already enfeebled government with accusations of cowardice and treason? The experience of events after the Second World War, when a totally defeated Germany was occupied and administered for several years before independent German institutions appeared again, might be cited as a ground for believing that Ebert and his colleagues were wrong to act so cautiously in 1919, and that complete disaster might have been preferable to prolonged agony at the hands of the peace-makers. Certainly no atmosphere of peace descended on Germany with the signing of the treaty; if anything, hostility to the victor powers became more marked, and was reinforced by hatred for those at home regarded as tools of the enemy.

Yet, even with the advantage of hindsight, the arguments in favour of last-ditch resistance do not stand up to very close scrutiny. In 1945 Germany was totally defeated. There could be no question of having been tricked or betrayed into peace. In the summer of 1919 a successful Allied invasion of the country would still have been blamed on the duplicity of Wilson, the treason of the revolutionaries and the weakness of the moderate political parties. Then again, there is no evidence that the Allies intended to take responsibility for the government of Germany as they were compelled to do after 1945. President Wilson and his colleagues in Paris wished simply to force the German government to sign the treaty. The methods they intended to adopt would almost certainly have been successful. Marshal Foch claimed that his armies could not march immediately to Berlin, but must first advance to the line of the Weser and occupy the Main valley. Separate treaties could then be made with the South German states leaving Berlin isolated.[13] This would have given the Allies control of Germany's most vital industrial region, and would have implied that the recurrent German nightmare of national dismemberment might become a reality. No German government could be expected to risk the unity of the Reich. Nor is there much reason to suppose that dismemberment would have produced a lasting peace. It should be remembered that, however unfavourable the treaty was for the future development of German democracy, there was no means of knowing that the new Republic would founder as a result. The Third French Republic had come into being under similar conditions of trial and had survived. Neither Ebert nor the Allied leaders could be expected to foresee that events in Germany would take such a different and catastrophic course.

[1] Burdick–Lutz, *Political Institutions*, p. 70.

[2] *Foreign Relations of the United States. The Paris Peace Conference 1919*, vol. XII (U.S.G.P.O., Washington, 1947) pp. 3–4.

[3] *Deutsche Nationalversammlung* (ed. Hölfron), vol. I, pp. 4–5. Translation as given in papers relating to the *Foreign Relations of the United States. The Paris Peace Conference 1919*, vol. XII (U.S.G.P.O., Washington, 1947) p. 9.

[4] Turner, *Stresemann*, p. 37.

[5] Earl of Swinton, *Sixty Years of Power*, p. 29.

[6] Graf Brockdorff-Rantzau, *Versailles*, p. 47. Speech to the German National Assembly, 14 February 1919.

[7] Keynes, *Economic Consequences*, p. 32.

[8] See, for example, the statements by Lord Brand in 'How a Banker Watched History Happen'.

[9] For a discussion of this subject see Holborn in *The Diplomats*, pp. 138–45, and Dickmann, 'Die Kriegsschuldfrage auf der Friedenskonferenz von Paris 1919'.

[10] See Geiss, 'The Outbreak of the First World War and German War Aims'.

[11] See Petzold, *Die Dolchstosslegende*, p. 27, and Wheeler-Bennett, *Hindenburg*, p. 238.

[12] Carsten, *Reichswehr*, pp. 40–2.

[13] Mantoux, *Les Deliberations du Conseil des Quatre*, vol. II, pp. 22–3, 69, and 430 ff. Also Zimmermann, *Deutsche Aussenpolitik*, pp. 61–3.

5 1919–1922: Years of Crisis and Uncertainty

ON 21 August 1919 Ebert, who had been acting as provisional President since the previous February, took the oath to the Constitution as Germany's first Republican head of state. The fact that he did not present himself for popular election as envisaged in the constitution illustrated the weakness of the new régime. Public opinion had been so outraged by the Versailles Treaty that an anti-Republican candidate might have defeated Ebert. Similarly, the Constituent National Assembly did not dissolve itself, but continued to function as Germany's legislature. The Weimar Coalition parties did not wish to face a parliamentary election.[1]

Public enthusiasm for the government was not increased when Matthias Erzberger – now Reich Finance Minister – introduced a comprehensive programme of taxation to deal with Germany's pressing financial problems. These had been inherited from the Imperial government, which had borrowed heavily during the war, and had been aggravated by the disturbed conditions after the revolution and the losses caused by the peace treaty. Erzberger was an energetic minister, and he gave Germany a coherent taxation system which placed the burden of sacrifice firmly on the wealthy. He imposed taxes on war profits, capital gains, inherited wealth and excess consumption. Income tax was graded to fall more severely on the rich, and was supplemented by a capital levy.[2] These measures, which were very advanced for their era, naturally aroused the fury of the well-to-do. Erzberger was accused of being simply a financial agent of Germany's enemies, squeezing money

Erzberger's programme of taxation

from the Germans for the benefit of the victor powers. A vitriolic campaign of public denunciation was whipped up against him, spearheaded by Karl Helfferich, a former Vice-Chancellor and financial expert under Wilhelm II. Erzberger was so discredited as a result that he had to retire from politics in the spring of 1920.

At almost the same time the Republic was rocked by the first serious attempt at counter-revolution since November 1918. This was the Kapp Putsch. Its major cause was discontent in the army. The Versailles Treaty required heavy reductions in Germany's armed forces. Many of the Freikorps formations recruited in 1919 to uphold internal order or protect Germany's eastern frontiers could expect to be disbanded. Their members faced unemployment. The feeling among most of their officers was fiercely hostile to the Republican government.

The commander of the Reichswehr district which included Berlin was General von Lüttwitz. He begun to conspire with a number of reactionary civilians, chief among whom was a former Prussian civil servant, Wolfgang Kapp, who had been associated with demands for an annexationist peace during the war. Also involved in the conspiracy was General Ludendorff. He had fled the country in terror after the revolution, but in February 1919 had returned to Berlin and established an anti-Republican salon there, frequented by reactionaries of various types.[3]

Matters came to a head in March 1920, when the Defence Minister, Noske, attempted to disband two naval brigades stationed near Berlin. On the night of 12/13 March these units marched into the capital unopposed. Noske and General Reinhardt wanted to offer resistance, but their military colleagues would not support them. General von Seeckt, the most influential staff officer in the Defence Ministry, spoke out firmly against the army involving itself in what he saw as a political battle. He put the interests of the army before his duty to defend the Government.[4]

President Ebert, Reich Chancellor Bauer and most of the cabinet fled the city and went to Stuttgart. The National Assembly joined them there. One member of the Government, Vice-Chancellor Schiffer of the Democratic Party, was left behind to watch events in Berlin.

The Kapp–Lüttwitz régime, called to power by the mutinous marine Freikorps, was quite incapable of any constructive policy. Collaboration between the military and civilian elements in the *coup* was notable for its absence, and what plans there were proved impossible to realise.[5] More important were the reactions to it and the results of its failure. Organised labour gave the most unequivocal demonstration of hostility to the Putsch. The trade unions called a general strike. In Berlin Kapp and Lüttwitz found themselves controlling a dead city. The civil service and the army were also unhelpful, but their attitude was less clearcut. Ministerial officials did not work for the new régime. General von Seeckt, who had become the most important man in the army after Reinhardt's humiliation, left his office and donned civilian clothes. Nevertheless, a group of his staff officers adopted a resolution declaring that they 'stood aloof' from events in Berlin, that they understood negotiations were going on between Kapp and the old (*sic*) administration and that they were willing to preserve law and order until a government which had the confidence of the nation was established. This was no ringing declaration of loyalty to the Republican ministry. Kapp and Lüttwitz expressed their thanks when it was communicated to them.[6] Even more disturbing for Ebert and Bauer was the fact that in some provincial areas army commanders were clearly in favour of Kapp, as was virtually the whole of the navy.

The Putsch also attracted sympathy from the two right-wing parties. The German Nationalists avoided any formal commitment to Kapp, but they issued a statement condemning the legal government for not holding parliamentary elections. Stresemann and his colleagues in the

German People's Party were quite favourably impressed with Kapp, and seemed ready to negotiate with him.[7] None of these overtures were of any help to the Putschists. As days went by it became clear that they could wield no effective authority. Kapp and Lüttwitz fled the country, leaving Bauer's government apparently triumphant.

The ignominious collapse of the Putsch ought to have been a victory for the Republic. The right-wing parties had been seriously compromised. Reactionary elements in the army and the civil service had revealed both their disloyalty and their impotence. Public opinion was overwhelmingly hostile to the Putsch. Yet most of the politicians and officials who might have feared reprisals managed to wriggle off the hook on which they had apparently impaled themselves. They owed their deliverance partly to confusion within Bauer's government and partly to a new fear of revolution from the left.

Bauer and his colleagues were prepared to take stern measures against Kapp's supporters, but were embarrassed to find that in Berlin Vice-Chancellor Schiffer and other coalition party members had apparently offered promises of leniency to the leaders of the Putsch.[8] Even more important were the attempts by militant elements in the labour movement to use resistance to Kapp as an excuse for revolutionary activity. The trade union leadership in Berlin tried to force Ebert to appoint a purely socialist government which would introduce immediate socialisation of industry and create a new Republican army. The President was able to resist these demands, but he could not save Reich Chancellor Bauer, who had to resign.

The new government was headed by Hermann Müller, another Social Democrat. Noske had been forced to give up the Defence Ministry. General Reinhardt had already resigned after his failure to protect the Government, and General von Seeckt became chief of the Reichswehr. Noske's successor was a right-wing Democrat called Otto Gessler.

He had no particular desire to impose civilian authority on the army, and von Seeckt was able to keep the officer corps aloof from Republican politics. No serious consequences overtook the army as the result of the Kapp Putsch. Indeed, some soldiers who had been loyal to the Republic fared worse than their mutinous superiors.[9]

Ruhr in 1920

Von Seeckt's position was made easier by outbreaks of left-wing violence in the Ruhr. It was thought that a Communist *coup* was imminent. As usual, the Communists were credited with more than they deserved. They had originally opposed trade union strike action against Kapp, claiming that the workers ought not to become involved in a clash between counter-revolutionary elements. Only when it became clear that the resistance to Kapp had overwhelming working-class support did the Communists change their tactics. Then they did all they could to exploit the strike, hoping to extend it into a demand for proletarian dictatorship. Even in this they had been forestalled. A spontaneous revolt broke out in the Ruhr in which Independent Social Democrats, anarcho-syndicalists and some supporters of the Majority Social Democratic Party were as important as the Communists.[10] Arms were distributed and barricades erected. The Reichswehr marched in to crush the insurgents, which it did with brutal efficiency.

KPD

revolt

The fighting in the Ruhr did no good to the cause of the Majority Social Democratic Party. Once again it seemed to be encouraging counter-revolutionary officers to suppress the working classes. The Independent Social Democrats gained in popularity as a result.

On the other hand, the demands of the trade unions and the fighting in the Ruhr scandalised the non-socialist parties in the coalition. The Centre, in particular, regretted its association with the general strike, and wanted to distance itself at once from revolutionary elements. One result of this was that Chancellor Müller agreed to call elections for a new Reichstag.

The Kapp Putsch has been seen as the turning point in Republican fortunes – the moment when democracy in Germany finally lost its way. It certainly demonstrated the Republic's weaknesses, but it may be doubted whether it was more than a symptom of diseases which already existed. Noske's fall diminished political control over the army, but this had never been very effective. In any case, von Seeckt, for all his desire to preserve the purity of his officer corps, was a cautious man, and his régime in the Bendlerstrasse did not encourage political adventures. So far as the German Nationalist Party was concerned it was chastened rather than encouraged by the failure of the Putsch, and was eager to disown it. Among both the DNVP and Stresemann's People's Party the view gained ground that power exercised according to the constitution should be the aim of the German Right. Indeed, in many ways the worst result of the Putsch was the 1920 elections.

Held on 6 June 1920, they were a fresh disaster for the Republican parties. The SPD, Democrats and Centre between them lost eight of the nineteen million votes they had mustered at the National Assembly elections eighteen months earlier. They were now in a minority, although their opponents were completely split.

On the left, the Independent Social Democrats had begun to approach the SPD in size and electoral support. On the right Stresemann's People's Party trebled its vote and returned sixty-five Reichstag deputies; the German Nationalists polled over a million more votes than in 1918 and returned seventy-five deputies.

Defeat at the polls caused Chancellor Müller to resign. The SPD, the party most committed to supporting the Republic, left the Government. An elderly but respected leader of the Centre Party, Fehrenbach, formed a new cabinet, which included representatives of Stresemann's People's Party. Stresemann himself became chairman of the Reichstag's Foreign Affairs Committee.

Fehrenbach's ministry was beset with diplomatic and economic problems. Germany's former enemies accused her of defaulting on her reparations obligations and of evading the disarmament clauses in the Versailles Treaty. There was truth in both claims, but the Government in Berlin could not always help itself.

Reparations

So far as reparations were concerned, the Germans had been left in apprehensive uncertainty about the extent of their indebtedness. In 1919 the Allies could not agree on a total figure which would be large enough to appease their own public and small enough to give the Germans even a theoretical chance of paying it. The task of setting a final figure was given to an inter-Allied Reparations Commission, and in the meantime Germany had to make large deliveries of gold, convertible currency, goods and raw materials. It was realised in London and Paris that the Germans would have difficulty in meeting projected Allied reparations demands. France and Britain had themselves incurred heavy debts to the U.S.A. during the war, and the British, in particular, would have been willing to treat Germany more leniently if inter-Allied indebtedness were reduced. From the very first, however, the Americans refused to consider such a solution. The fact that America had avoided accepting any obligation to support a system of international security also helped to throw the French and the British back on a strict interpretation of the Peace Treaty as the best guarantee of their safety. High protective tariffs in the United States made European economic reconstruction even more difficult. A number of attempts were made to reach an agreement over reparations between Germany and the Allies, but they all failed.

Disarmament

On the question of disarmament the Germans had been slow to fulfil their obligations, and the Reichswehr leaders undoubtedly hoped to maintain larger forces than those envisaged in the Treaty. General Seeckt and his colleagues were to become practised in the arts of evasion. Most Reich governments closed their eyes to such activities, illegal though they were. Nevertheless, in some cases they simply lacked the power to meet Allied requirements, being unable, for instance, to dissolve large 'Home Guard' forces retained by the right-wing government in Bavaria.

The crisis over reparations and disarmament came to a head in the spring of 1921. On 27 April the Allied Reparations Commission finally set the total German reparations debt at 132 thousand million gold marks – a figure lower than some originally mentioned by the Allies, but considerably more than those offered by the Germans.

On 5 May 1921 the Allies delivered an ultimatum. Germany had to accept an Allied schedule of reparations payments and complete her disarmament. She should bring men designated as war criminals to trial. If these terms were not accepted the Allies would occupy the Ruhr – Germany's most important industrial complex. A number of west German cities had already been occupied in connexion with an earlier ultimatum, and the Germans had no reason to hope that they were faced with an idle threat.

Fehrenbach had already resigned when the ultimatum was delivered. His successor was a man of much more forceful character. This was Josef Wirth, also of the Centre Party. In some ways he was the most attractive leader the Republic had produced since its foundation. He certainly earned the distinction of being Germany's youngest Chancellor since that office had been established in 1871. His appointment marked a shift away from the right-ward trend in German politics, since Stresemann's People's Party left the Government, and the Social Democrats rejoined the coalition.

Coming from Baden, in the German south-west, Wirth represented the more democratic and socially reformist tendency within the Centre Party. As finance minister in Fehrenbach's cabinet he had aroused displeasure among right-wing parties for his stress on direct taxation. His grasp of financial technicalities was to stand him in good stead when grappling with reparations problems. Unlike many other Centre Party politicians he had no employment other than politics, to which he devoted himself with great energy. His attractive personality, parliamentary skill and direct but effective technique as a platform speaker had aided his meteoric rise from a school-teaching post in Baden to the summit of German political life. In many ways he was an example of the best the Weimar Republic could provide; his career would have been impossible under the old Empire. By the same token, his bluff manner and convivial disposition aroused distaste among those who preferred the more colourless behaviour of Imperial officials.

Wirth's name is associated above all with the policy known as 'fulfilment'. He was loyal to the Republic and believed that with careful and clever diplomacy Germany could improve her position in the world. 'Patience, more patience and still more patience' was his recipe for success, and it was sensible advice at a time when Germany was isolated and defenceless.[11] This did not mean that he wanted to surrender to Germany's enemies. On the contrary, he hoped that by adopting a less obstructive attitude than earlier governments he could weaken the united Allied front against Germany and modify the conditions imposed upon her.

At home Wirth's aim was to inaugurate a policy of reconstruction and reconciliation, laying stress on loyalty to the Republican constitution. 'He who loves his country will follow the flag of the German Republic' was his slogan.[12] It was a view which had not previously been accepted by all his Centre Party colleagues and was even less attractive to many members of Stresemann's People's Party. Yet, as the political situation developed without either a socialist revolution or a monarchist restoration, more and more of the bourgeois politicians were coming to feel that their best policy would be to come to terms with the Republic and work within its constitution. Stresemann, in particular, was unhappy at being excluded from power, and hoped to bring his party back into the Government when a favourable opportunity presented itself. It was unfortunate that the progressive devaluation of the currency, which had taken a sudden turn for the worse with the Allied ultimatum, was intensifying feelings of desperation among the public at large at a time when political leaders were more ready for compromise. Extremism on both the left and the right became more attractive to the man in the street as his economic condition worsened.

Violence in politics did not disappear with the end of the revolution. Nationalist fanatics were responsible for a number of outrages against prominent Republicans or persons whom they suspected of betraying secrets about clandestine military activity. In August 1921 a particularly shocking case occurred when Matthias Erzberger, the former Finance Minister, was assassinated in the Black Forest.

Initially, however, Wirth's fulfilment policy showed some good results. The Germans accepted the Allied ultimatum in an agreement signed in London on 11 May. The follow- *London* ing month the Bavarians were forced to disband their Home Guard. A number of Germans were brought to trial on war crimes charges. As was to be expected, the judgements were anything but harsh. Wirth made determined efforts to meet the Allied reparations demands, but here the difficulties *Reparations* facing him were too great to be overcome. German currency was losing its value all the time. Despite more stringent taxation measures the budget could not be balanced. The Allied Powers demanded major reforms in German domestic policy to enable the currency to be stabilised. Reparations should then be paid for out of a budgetary surplus. It was the German case that no realistic reform could be carried out while the country was burdened with such heavy reparations debts. The need to make large transfers of gold and convertible currency from Germany to the creditor nations was a large strain on Germany's reserves and weakened the mark. This in turn meant that no credit was forthcoming from abroad because foreign bankers did not believe financial stability could be achieved while the country was having to face such a large reparations burden.

On the whole it seems clear that – whatever the theoretical merits of the Allied case – in practice the Germans were right. Soon even Wirth's efforts over reparations failed. Germany had to declare that she would be unable to make the payments due at the beginning of 1922. 'Fulfilment' seemed to be leading Germany into a blind alley.

Wirth had quickly begun to lose faith in the possibility of concessions from Britain and France, although he had not renounced fulfilment. Instead he switched his attention to the east, hoping to strengthen Germany's diplomatic position by drawing closer to Soviet Russia. Moves for a better relationship with Lenin's Bolshevik government had been going on for some time. As early as 6 May 1921 the Germans signed a commercial agreement with Russia. It was not very wide in scope, but it confirmed German *de jure* recognition of the Soviet régime and envisaged an increase in trade between the two countries.

This Eastern policy was not just commercial. The German army was also involved. General von Seeckt had already authorised contacts with the Russians with a view to possible collaboration. Russia was not a signatory of the Versailles peace settlement. Arrangements with her might enable the Reichswehr to evade some of the restrictions put upon it by the Western Powers. By using Russian help the German army hoped to be able to keep abreast of developments in air and tank warfare, despite the prohibitions on such activities imposed by Versailles. Military personnel could be trained and forbidden armaments produced under Soviet auspices. In return the Russians would benefit from German technical help and administrative expertise.

The practical collaboration which von Seeckt hoped to achieve by making arrangements with the Russians did not in his case imply the slightest fondness for Communism or willingness to compromise with it in Germany. But there were on both the extreme left and the nationalist right in Germany men who believed that their country's future lay in an arrangement with the East. Hatred of Western democracy and plutocratic capitalism – the enemies which had apparently caused Germany's downfall – encouraged a feeling of solidarity between the outcasts of Europe: Germany and Russia.

In the German Foreign Ministry the most enthusiastic supporter of a pro-Russian policy was the head of the Eastern Division, Count Ago von Maltzan. In the summer of 1921 he and Wirth agreed that closer relations with the Soviet Union ought to be the primary aim of German diplomacy.[13] The Germans could thereby hope to gain more room for manœuvre in foreign affairs. There was also a defensive aspect to Wirth's policy. The Soviet government was trying to normalise relations with the West. Germany would thus have competition from Britain and France in the race for Russian favours. Lloyd George, in particular, became very interested in the expansion of Anglo-Russian trade. The British Prime Minister had promised Britain's soldiers a 'world fit for heroes to live in' when they returned from the war. Instead they found a stagnating economy and large-scale unemployment. Favourable terms of trade with Russia would brighten the prospect. For their part the French were eager to obtain compensation from Russia for the Tsarist loans repudiated by the Bolshevik government. As a lever to obtain Soviet compliance on both trade and debt questions the Western Allies might hope to use Article 116 of the Versailles Treaty, which reserved to Russia the right to make reparations demands against Germany for damage done during the war.

Furthermore, from the German military viewpoint it was

most unlikely that a consortium in which Britain and France
exerted much influence would tolerate secret German arms
projects. Although Wirth made it his business not to enquire
too closely into von Seeckt's dealings with the Red Army,
he certainly knew that contacts existed. It was through his
intervention that secret funds were made available to the
Reichswehr for arms projects in Russia.[14] Wirth and von
Maltzan both felt that the Russian connexion was too
valuable to be allowed to go by default.

Matters came to a head when Lloyd George persuaded
his allies to call a European Economic Conference at Genoa
in April 1922. Russia and Germany were both invited; the
first time that the two outsiders in European politics had sat
together at an international conference. The Soviet government did not have high hopes of gaining commercial
advantages from Britain and France at Genoa. It therefore
sent representatives to Berlin in an attempt to reach a formal
agreement with the German government before the
conference began. The Russian Foreign Minister, Chicherin,
personally stopped off in the German capital to ensure the
success of this project. A protocol was drawn up by
Chicherin and von Maltzan which was virtually a treaty of
friendship between the two countries.[15]

No formal agreement was made owing to reservations
about association with Soviet Russia among Wirth's
political colleagues. President Ebert had always disliked the
Bolsheviks and had no desire to forge links with them. He
had not been fully informed of Germany's moves towards
Russia. Rathenau, the Foreign Minister, was also reluctant
to announce a treaty with Russia before the Genoa Conference because this might damage Germany's relations
with the Western Powers. Rathenau harboured a faint hope
that the conference might eventually lead to Allied concessions over reparations.

Yet when the German delegation – headed by Wirth and
Rathenau – went to Genoa they found that Lloyd George

was more eager to talk to the Russians than to them. It seemed that a scheme might be being worked out which would be prejudicial to German interests, and the Soviet delegation did all it could to heighten this impression when talking to the Germans.[16]

At 2 a.m. on 16 April von Maltzan suddenly appeared in Rathenau's hotel room and told him that Chicherin was inviting the German delegation to a meeting at Rapallo later in the day. Rathenau wanted to use this information as a lever to encourage Lloyd George to negotiate with the Germans, but Wirth and von Maltzan insisted that Chicherin's offer be accepted. By that evening a Treaty of Friendship had been concluded between the German and Soviet delegations. It safeguarded the Germans from any future Russian claims under the Versailles Treaty and ensured that Germany would enjoy most-favoured-nation treatment in its trade relations with Russia. There was no secret military protocol attached to the Rapallo Treaty, but its conclusion meant that collaboration between the Red Army and the Reichswehr was likely to be intensified, and this was in fact the case.[17]

News of the agreement naturally caused a sensation at Genoa and it was blamed for the meagre results produced by the conference. The French eagerly denounced German duplicity and Lloyd George was also indignant. There is no good reason to suppose that the Germans lost much by their action. Lloyd George did not use Rapallo as an excuse for breaking up the Genoa Conference. On the contrary, he treated the Germans with more consideration, hoping they might help him gain concessions from Russia. The conference had never offered much chance of solving Germany's financial problems. British and American financial experts present at Genoa made it clear that an international loan to stabilise Germany's currency could only be raised if there was some prospect of a reparations settlement. Yet the French would not allow reparations to be put on the agenda at Genoa.[18]

Rapallo was the first real attempt by the Germans to take the initiative in foreign affairs and overcome their isolation. In many ways it was successful; the Russo-German contacts forged by the treaty continued and were the basis for more important economic co-operation later on. The fact that Germany had a link with Moscow gave her diplomatic advantages three years afterwards when she came to bargain with the West in a more favourable atmosphere. The military collaboration between the Reichswehr and the Red Army brought technical benefits to the former which were of considerable value when the army was rapidly expanded by Hitler in the 1930s. On the other hand, the Russo-German alignment alone could never be enough to overcome Germany's weakness *vis-à-vis* her former enemies. It may have encouraged the Germans to think that they could exert more pressure on Poland – with whom they had very bad relations for most of the 1920s – than was in fact the case. The Reichswehr could never become powerful enough to challenge Germany's conquerors by secret rearmament alone. It was the transformed diplomatic climate of the post-depression period which enabled Hitler to exploit opportunities never given to Republican politicians.

In May 1922 Wirth, after his return from Genoa, had completed a year in office as Chancellor – the longest run any leader had achieved since the Republic was founded. His colleagues in the Centre Party could feel that their Chancellor had extricated Germany from the period of crisis in which he had assumed power. Even if the conferences at Genoa had not led to any result they did seem to show a willingness on the part of other powers to listen to Germany's point of view. As one Centre Party newspaper put it: 'a year ago they dictated to us; now they negotiate'.[19]

Indeed, the early summer months of 1922 seemed remarkably calm. Germany had a stable coalition into which one of the opposition parties, Stresemann's DVP,

1*a*. The New Government,
10 November 1918
From left to right: Emil Barth,
Otto Landsberg, Friedrich
Ebert, Hugo Haase, Wilhelm
Dittmann and Philipp
Scheidemann

1*b*. Friedrich Ebert,
1871–1925
President of the Republic,
1919–1925

2. Berlin, January 1919: the aftermath of street fighting

3. Berlin, January 1919: Government troops and rebels meet for a parley

4a. Captain Ehrhardt, the *Freikorps* leader, whose unit played a prominent part in the Kapp *Putsch* (marked with a cross)

4b. Dr Josef Wirth, 1879–1956

4c. Dr Gustav Stresemann, 1878–19[

5. Field-Marshal Paul von Hindenburg, 1847–1934, President of the Republic, 1925–1934, seen reviewing troops with Defence Minister Gessler and General von Seeckt. Hindenburg is on the left

6. Hitler and von Pfeffer, chief of the SA, in 1928

7. Dr Heinrich Brüning (1885–) addressing a rally supporting Hindenburg
in the Presidential election, 1932

8a. Franz von Papen (1879–).
Papen is on the right next to
Otto Meissner, the President's
State Secretary

8b. General Kurt von
Schleicher, 1882–1934.
Schleicher was murdered by
the Nazis on 30th June 1934

was doing its best to enter. Territorial disputes had been settled with Poland and Denmark. The reparations issue was hanging fire. But it was a calm before the storm.

On 24 June Foreign Minister Rathenau was murdered by nationalist youths. This act was well summed up by Stresemann in the remark:

> Political work often seems to me to be a labour of Sisyphus. Whenever one has rolled the stone up far enough so that one can believe in a stabilization of the general situation, then some fanatic plunges us into a new misfortune.[20]

Germany suffered a severe loss of international prestige with Rathenau's death. The Mark fell on world exchanges. In Berlin, Wirth reacted fiercely to the outrage and presented the Reichstag with the Law to Defend the Republic, giving the Government wide powers against enemies of the constitution. The Socialist trade unions organised strikes and demonstrations.

These events did not strengthen the coalition. Wirth's colleagues in the Centre Party, although shocked at Rathenau's murder, did not wish to embark on a campaign of radicalism. They disliked the militancy of Socialist trade unions. Catholic unions did not participate in the strikes. The fact was that the SPD was losing the sympathy of its coalition partners. It was clear in the summer of 1922 that the Independent Socialists and the SPD were moving closer together. Those Independents who had not gone over to the Communists were preparing to rejoin the SPD. After Rathenau's murder the two parties made a parliamentary alliance in the Reichstag. Social Democracy began to take on a more militant appearance.

At the same time Stresemann's People's Party was making strenuous efforts to conciliate the Democrats and Centre. When Rathenau was murdered Stresemann took the opportunity to align the DVP more firmly behind the Republican constitution than ever before. Though not

D

finally renouncing monarchism it adopted a resolution declaring:

The dispute over the form of government must be put aside during our Fatherland's time of distress. We are of the conviction that the reconstruction of Germany is only possible within the framework of the Republican constitution.[21]

Stresemann went further and persuaded a large section of his supporters to vote for the controversial Law to Defend the Republic. Immediately afterwards it was agreed in principle that the Centre, Democrat and People's Party delegations in the Reichstag should consult together on important issues. This combination was to be given the high-sounding title of an 'Alliance of the constitutionally loyal middle' (*Verfassungstreue Mitte*).

In September the SPD and the Independents finally merged. The Social Democratic Party thus became stronger in the Reichstag. Wirth was not unhappy about this development, since he had always worked well with the SPD. But his party grew restive and pressed for concessions to Stresemann. In November it insisted that the People's Party be admitted to the cabinet. Wirth had to resign.

A much more conservative cabinet was formed by Dr Wilhelm Cuno. Cuno was a former official of Wilhelm II who had become head of the Hamburg-America shipping line. His appointment was a retrograde step; it lessened the responsibility of parliamentary parties for the actions of the executive. Cuno's choice of ministers reflected a predilection for non-party 'experts' as against men of distinction in the Reichstag. His cabinet included a general, an ambassador, and the mayor of Essen, Hans Luther, who later described himself in his memoirs as a 'politician without a party'.

Cuno was quickly faced with a major crisis. The French government, led by the particularly intransigent M.

Poincaré, was not prepared to prevaricate further on the question of reparations. German industry seemed to be booming under inflationary conditions, and the French saw no reason why Germany should not meet her obligations to the Allies. At the end of December the French complained that Germany was defaulting on deliveries of telegraph poles. The Reparations Commission upheld their claim. On 11 January the French and the Belgians informed Cuno's government that they were sending a technical control commission to the Ruhr to supervise reparations deliveries. The occupation of Germany's most important industrial complex had begun.

[1] Turner, *Stresemann*, p. 47.

[2] Epstein, *Matthias Erzberger*, pp. 338–48.

[3] Goodspeed, *Ludendorff*, pp. 220–5.

[4] Carsten, *Reichswehr*, pp. 79, 92–3. Also Erger, *Kapp–Lüttwitz-Putsch*, p. 143.

[5] Gordon, *Reichswehr*, pp. 110–11.

[6] Carsten, *Reichswehr*, p. 82.

[7] Turner, *Stresemann*, p. 52.

[8] Erger, *Kapp–Lüttwitz–Putsch*, p. 282.

[9] Carsten, *Reichswehr*, pp. 95–6.

[10] Angress, *Stillborn Revolution*, p. 45.

[11] Brecht, *Aus nächster Nähe*, p. 344.

[12] Ibid. p. 345.

[13] Helbig, *Rapallopolitik*, p. 57.

[14] Freund, *Unholy Alliance*, p. 97; Helbig, *Rapallopolitik*, pp. 57–8; Carsten, *Reichswehr*, pp. 138, 141–2.

[15] Helbig, *Rapallopolitik*, pp. 77–83.

[16] Freund, *Unholy Alliance*, p. 116. Helbig, *Rapallopolitik*, pp. 89–90 states that the French were in fact suggesting to the Russians an arrangement whereby Russian repayment of Czarist debts should be covered by German reparations. The Russians seem to have been willing to consider repayment of the debts, but in return demanded Allied compensation for damage caused by their intervention against the Bolsheviks in the Russian civil war. The differences between the two sides proved impossible to overcome.

[17] For descriptions of the events at Rapallo see Freund, *Unholy Alliance*, pp. 115–19; Helbig, *Rapallopolitik*, pp. 88 ff.; Kessler, *Walther Rathenau*, pp. 319–59.

[18] Erdmann, 'Deutschland, Rapallo und der Westen', pp. 151–2.

[19] Morsey, *Zentrumspartei*, p. 450.

[20] Turner, *Stresemann*, pp. 97–8.

[21] Ibid. p. 99.

6 Hitler and Republican Instability

As Germany's reparations problems grew more critical her internal security was being threatened by developments in Bavaria. Ever since the Kapp Putsch in March 1920, when the government in Munich had been entrusted to a monarchist official, Gustav von Kahr, Bavaria had become a centre for anti-Republican extremists.

The November revolution and the Munich Soviet Republic in April 1919 had been a great psychological shock to the propertied classes in Bavaria. Before the war their country had enjoyed political stability. The largest political party had been the Bavarian section of the Roman Catholic Centre. This had given fairly loyal – if sometimes fractious – support to the ministers appointed by Bavaria's Wittelsbach monarchs. After the November revolution a new organisation calling itself the Bavarian People's Party was established. It hoped to unite all conservative, Christian elements in the state, but in practice it inherited the supporters and most of the leaders of the old Bavarian Centre. On a national level it worked together with the Centre Party, and one of its members became a minister in the Weimar Coalition government. However, such collaboration soon became difficult. The new era had ushered in all sorts of unpleasant surprises for the Bavarians, not the least of which was the Weimar Constitution itself. It robbed them of the special rights they had enjoyed under the old Empire. Although these were not of great practical importance, their loss was wounding to Bavarian pride. Politically more significant was the centralising activity of Matthias Erzberger, whose tax-gathering techniques and obvious distaste for local privileges aroused anger south of the Main. The fact that he was a leader of the Centre Party strained the BVP/Centre association to breaking point, and in January 1920 the Bavarian People's Party disassociated itself from its Catholic colleagues in the rest of Germany. Its minister in the Berlin government had to resign.[1]

A further bone of contention between Munich and Berlin was the hospitality shown by the Bavarian government to private para-military organisations known as Patriotic Leagues (*Vaterländische Verbände*). These were often the remnants of former Freikorps units which had not been incorporated in the Reichswehr. They were generally anti-Republican in character and indulged in counter-revolutionary plots. The Bavarian army and police authorities turned a blind eye to the Leagues' activities and sometimes actively supported them. Von Kahr's régime also shielded murder gangs which liquidated those suspected of revealing secret arms caches to officials in Berlin or representatives of the Western Allies.

Certainly the administration of police authority in Bavaria was very one-sided. Von Kahr's Police President in Munich was Ernst Pöhner, a man who sincerely believed that the moral fibre of Germany had been undermined by the November revolution. He did all he could to support those who would fight Marxism and democracy. His attitude to the Republic is well illustrated in a conversation with a senior Reich official sent to investigate the Bavarian situation in February 1921.

Pöhner began by sneering violently at the Berlin government, which, he claimed, was no government at all. In Munich everyone was ready to die for von Kahr; who would die for Ebert or Fehrenbach (the Reich Chancellor) or Gessler? He went on to describe the way in which he thought left-wing opponents should be treated by strong governments. If a strike was called in Berlin the government there would negotiate to try and end it. That was useless. Pöhner explained how he would deal with such a situation:

You call the strike leaders together for a meeting and demand that the work be resumed next day. If the first says no you shoot him and ask the second. If he says no you shoot him too. Then the third who will say yes. Then you have a total of two dead; using your negotiation methods there would be weeks of fighting with thousands dead.[2]

One beneficiary of such official attitudes in Bavaria was Adolf Hitler. He made his start in politics under the auspices of the Bavarian army. Bavaria was the school in which he learned his trade as a demagogue and party leader. The organisation he forged in these years was to carry him to power in Germany as a whole.

Born in 1889 in Braunau, on the Austrian side of the frontier with Bavaria, Hitler came from an unspectacular but hardly proletarian home. His father was a customs official, whose mother had only married some time after he had been born. Later on a great deal was made of the mystery surrounding Hitler's paternal grandfather. The possibility existed that he might actually have been a Jew. It was also pointed out that Hitler's father's name ought to have been that of his mother – Schickelgrüber. Since 'Heil Schickelgrüber' would hardly have been a rousing political slogan this was used as a propaganda weapon against the Nazi leader. In fact Adolf Hitler himself was quite legitimate and his name beyond question. Doubts concerning his ancestry were embarrassing to a politician propagating theories about racial purity, but there was no concrete proof that he had Jewish forebears.[3]

The importance attached to this point was symptomatic of the anti-semitic atmosphere which seems to surround Hitler from his earliest recorded youth. The period before the First World War had seen a resurgence of this ancient prejudice in many parts of Central and Eastern Europe. It was bound up with a wider reaction against economic and political liberalism with which the Jews, who had benefited from the trend towards legal equality, were sometimes associated.

Anti-semitism had originally owed a great deal of its force to religious hostility felt by Christians for Jews. But in the nineteenth century new and apparently more 'scientific' theories began to appear, according to which Jews were regarded as racially distinct from other Europeans. In fact such arguments had no scientific basis. Many of their supporters specifically denied the value of reason, preferring more emotional guides to action. Nevertheless, the belief that peoples were organic growths and that alien races would weaken or destroy them seemed more 'modern' than an attack on Jews as the enemies of Christianity. It also possessed the advantage of condemning all people of Jewish racial origin, no matter what their religious beliefs.

Tales of a Jewish 'world conspiracy' were already a common ingredient of anti-semitic literature before the First World War. One notorious description of mysterious Jewish cabals and plots against Christian society came to be known as the *Protocols of the Elders of Zion*. Of uncertain origin, it was enthusiastically disseminated by Russian anti-semites before the First World War, and after Tsarism collapsed in 1917 it was exported to the West by White Russian refugees.[4]

In pre-war Germany organised political anti-semitism was not successful as a separate political movement, but anti-semitic attitudes began to permeate apparently respectable movements such as the Pan-German League and the German Farmers' Association.[5] Racialist – or *Völkisch** – beliefs were current among middle-class youth dissatisfied with the achievements of united Germany and seeking a purer form of state than that represented by the Wilhelmine

* Völkisch implied racial membership of and identification with the *Volk* (folk) who constituted a nation.

Empire. Owing to pogroms in Russia against Jewish communities many Russian Jews fled to the West, and some of them settled in Germany. Their numbers were often exaggerated, but it was widely believed that such 'Eastern Jews' were a subversive influence, especially among university students.[6] In Austria-Hungary Jewish populations in Vienna and Budapest were easy targets for racialists' abuse.

It was to Vienna that Hitler had gone as a young man, after a period of schooling in Linz. He wanted to study art, but was unable to qualify for the drawing academy. Instead he spent several years drifting aimlessly in the Austrian capital, dabbling in art and discussing politics with his Bohemian acquaintances.

In 1913 he left Austria and went to Munich. When the war broke out in August 1914 he volunteered for the Bavarian army, having listened amidst a jubilant crowd to King Ludwig III declaring war against France and Russia. He was a good soldier, even if he did not rise above the rank of corporal. Serving on the Western Front, he was awarded the Iron Cross, first and second class. It seems that Hitler was very much happier in the army than he had been as a civilian; the organised chaos of war – so horrifying to most men – simply provided him with a sense of purpose he had previously lacked.[7]

Germany's defeat came to him as a moral and physical shock. When the war ended he was in a military hospital recovering from the effects of a gas attack.[8] On his recovery he found himself in barracks in Munich. The atmosphere there was very different from that at the front. Many soldiers were simply staying in uniform to keep a roof over their heads. Authority in the Bavarian army was now shared uneasily between officers and Soldiers' Councils. In Munich the latter had the upper hand. April 1919 saw the proclamation of a Soviet Republic, which caused more dissension among the soldiers. Hitler does not seem to have participated in the conflicts which occurred at that time, though he must have been only too aware of them. Like many of his colleagues he remained neutral, possibly donning a red arm-band when it seemed necessary, but refusing to join the Red Army.[9] When Munich was taken over by the 'White' forces – representing the legal government – Hitler was among many soldiers arrested on suspicion of complicity with the Communists. Testimony from some of his officers led to his release, and he seems to have provided the occupying authorities with information about revolutionary goings-on in the barracks.

The old officers in the Bavarian army had been shocked and humiliated by the November revolution and its consequences. They owed their return to Munich to Noske's forces from north Germany, and this was a further affront to their military pride. In their view the German people as a whole was demoralised and unless it could be made to pull itself together the country was bound to fall into the arms of Bolshevism.

They were determined to create an army loyal to its officers and free of 'subversive' elements. They wanted to restore discipline and morale. This had to be done by careful selection of personnel and by political indoctrination or 'enlightenment'. A section of the army staff in Munich was set up to organise lectures and courses of instruction to explain the causes of the revolution to politically un-educated soldiers. The officers who set up such courses were not themselves very sophisticated politically, and their attitude towards Germany's problems largely coincided with those of the nationalist opponents of the Republic. In particular they were eager to deny the charge that Imperial Germany was responsible for starting the Great War.

Hitler was selected for training as a political educator. He aroused the interest of his instructors – among whom there was at least one distinguished university professor – by his rhetorical talent and his determined anti-semitism. This latter characteristic was by no means unattractive to his superiors. The Munich Soviet Republic was widely believed to have been the work of Eastern Jews, and several leading participants in it actually had been of Jewish origin.* Hostility to Jews was therefore equated with loyalty to 'law and order' by the Army leaders.

The head of the press and propaganda department of the Bavarian Army Command, Captain Mayr, was an enthusiastic anti-semite. He received good reports of Hitler's propaganda activity among returning German prisoners of war and in other units. So Hitler was entrusted with more sophisticated tasks. Mayr's organisation kept watch on all political activities in Munich, hoping thereby to influence civilian as well as military opinion in a suitable direction. One of the political groups in which Mayr became interested was an obscure body called the German Workers' Party (DAP). In September 1919 Hitler was sent to one of its meetings. His demeanour impressed the party's leaders and he was asked to become a member. It was to be the beginning of a new career.[10]

The German Workers' Party itself had made no impact on Munich at all when Hitler joined it. Its founder was a railway worker called Anton Drexler, a man unfit for military service who had felt it his duty in the closing stages of the war to exhort his working-class comrades to support the war effort and struggle on for a victorious peace. The party's aim was to put German workers under German leadership and ensure them freedom from exploitation without going so far as to socialise industry. Employers' property should be respected so long as they did not abuse it. There should be a clear distinction between workers and 'proletariat'. The skilled and the diligent should be given the opportunity to identify themselves with the middle class.[11] After the fall of the Soviet Republic in May 1919 the

* There were, of course, plenty of native Bavarians in the Soviets, and the local Jewish community was overwhelmingly opposed to the revolution. But such facts were ignored at the time.

DAP also began to stress the anti-semitic element in its appeal. Nevertheless, it was still an unsuccessful and insignificant party when Hitler visited it on 12 September 1919.

Hitler afterwards claimed that he was the party's seventh member, but this is certainly untrue.[12] It is much more likely that he referred to his membership of the party's executive committee, to which he was almost immediately elected. Hitler's main task in the party was that for which he had been trained in the army: propaganda. He rapidly revealed himself to be the most effective orator within the ranks of the DAP.[13] On 24 February 1920 the party organised its first really large meeting in the Munich Hofbräuhaus – which had been a communist stronghold in the days of the Soviet Republic. Hitler was chosen to read out the terms of a new twenty-five-point party programme. The DAP also changed its name and became known as the National Socialist German Workers' Party, a title probably chosen to express solidarity with similarly named organisations in Germany, Austria and the Sudetenland.[14] From this time onwards the party began to make some impact on Munich and its environs, although it remained virtually unknown to the world at large.[15]

The party's new programme was a mixture of pan-German nationalism, racial exclusiveness and a resentful hostility to big business. It demanded a Greater German Reich and more land upon which to settle the country's surplus population. Citizenship should be restricted to people of German racial origin; aliens could not enjoy such rights, and Jews could never be citizens. The immigration of aliens into Germany should be stopped and those who had come into the country since August 1914 should be required to leave. The party did not specifically demand the abolition of parliamentary rule, but the corruption of parliamentary parties was attacked, as was Roman Law, which was to be replaced by a German Common Law. The press was to be cleansed of alien elements. Education was to be organised to disseminate respect for the State and build up a healthy nation. Religion would be tolerated as long as it did not threaten to undermine the State or offend German racial morals. The country should have a strong central government.

None of these ideas was original. Some points in the programme even bore a resemblance to sections in the Weimar Constitution, although it is hardly likely that this was intentional.[16] The desire for equality with other powers was a commonplace in 1920 and would have been accepted by nearly everyone. Greater Germany was a traditional nationalist design with its roots in the period before Bismarck. More adventurous was the claim that Germany should gain land upon which to settle her excess population, but that had been part of the Pan-German League's programme during the war.[17] Indeed, the Nazis were vague about this aspect of their policy, since they evidently considered it to refer to overseas colonies. The eastern orientation of Hitler's colonial policy set out in *Mein Kampf* was absent from the earliest objectives of the Nazi Party.[18] Attacks on Roman Law as a Jewish institution were also conventional in anti-semitic circles. Sections on religion and centralised government were at least partly an expression of nationalist hostility to Catholic Bavarian separatism, against which Hitler and his colleagues were vigorously polemicising.

On the social and economic plane the party's policy was largely indebted to the work of its idiosyncratic economic theorist, Gottfried Feder. Feder was obsessed with the belief that finance capital – money invested to produce profit through interest – lay at the root of all society's problems. He regarded banks as the equivalent of robber barons in the Middle Ages, and thought that their influence should be greatly restricted. This did not mean, however, that he believed in the nationalisation of private property. On the contrary, he was often at pains to stress his respect for property and for the enterprise of the individual business-man.[19] Feder reflected the hostility to large-scale capitalism felt by many Germans in what might be described as the old middle class – officials, independent businessmen, shop-keepers, craftsmen and farmers.

It was this utopian socialism of the small proprietor that underlay the social elements in the Nazi programme. Each citizen had a duty to work creatively for the common good. The 'tyranny of interest' had to be broken. War profiteers were to be treated as criminals, industrial trusts should be nationalised and there should be profit-sharing in industry. Chain department stores were to be expropriated and leased to local shopkeepers. Despite the apparently revolutionary aspects of this programme it implied no large-scale attack on property for the benefit of the working classes. Point sixteen of the policy statement demanded the creation of a healthy middle class, by which was clearly meant the skilled craftsman, the farmer, the shopkeeper, small businessman and the salaried employee. It was precisely these groups which were thought to have suffered most severely during the war, and who were threatened most severely by the inflation which followed it.

Some space has been devoted to an account of this programme, because the description of Hitler's followers as members of a 'socialist' workers' party has caused some confusion. The Nazi Party did not appeal only – or indeed mainly – to workers, and its socialism was of a kind which involved state controls but no major redistribution of wealth. This is not to suggest that it was ever the tool of big business or that it appealed exclusively to an ill-defined group called the lower middle class. But Hitler never allowed it to come into serious conflict with powerful vested interests among Germany's propertied classes, unless the Jews could be counted as such. His party never had a markedly proletarian character and when, later in the 1920s, attempts were made to stress its socially revolutionary tendencies, he successfully prevented National Socialism from being marked out as a specifically anti-capitalist movement.

Hitler himself was almost certainly not the author of the party programme, and in the years which followed he did not always seem very concerned about its fulfilment. He is supposed to have told Hermann Rauschning that 'it is for the masses. It points the direction of some of our endeavours – neither more nor less – it is like the dogma of the Church.'[20] Since Hitler admired the Church chiefly for the techniques with which it influenced the masses, this last comment reinforces an impression of cynicism towards the declared aims of his party. Yet there is no reason to assume that the Nazi programme did not coincide with Hitler's own political views. Some parts of it he regarded with more enthusiasm than others; this was to be expected. It is also not surprising that the social aspects of the programme – most of which were completely unrelated to the realities of German economic life – proved largely unworkable in practice. This is a fate not unknown to befall political programmes elsewhere. Indeed, if a party leader were only to be judged by the extent to which he carried out his promises, Hitler would have to be put in the highest class.

Two fundamental attitudes dominated Hitler's political career. The first was his hatred of the Jews, which never wavered from his earliest recorded statements until the day of his death in 1945. On 16 September 1919 he wrote to a soldier in his regiment:

Everything which makes men strive for higher things, whether it be religion, socialism, or democracy is for him (the Jew) merely a means to an end, to satisfy his lust for money and power. His influence will result in national race tuberculosis.[21]

By attributing to the Jews a lust for power Hitler was unconsciously revealing his own compulsive urges in the same direction, for the second and more important motivating force in his life was a desire to achieve and exercise power over others. He always firmly believed that it was necessary and morally justifiable for the strong to rule – and even to destroy – the weak. Although he was to owe his success to the way in which he aroused mass support, he spoke of the masses with open contempt; as 'feminine', fickle and incapable of decision or rational calculation. They had to be bullied, cajoled and deceived by strong-willed leaders if they were to be politically effective. For this reason the techniques of mass manipulation fascinated Hitler and he mastered them in a fashion unrivalled by any of his contemporaries.[22] In this process the individual points of the programme were not so important as the general climate of opinion to which it appealed.

As we have already seen, the lost war and the disappointing peace had left many Germans feeling frustrated and resentful. Inflation, which had begun during the war and became rapidly worse after the revolution, was devaluing the salaries and savings of many who normally regarded themselves as safe from the economic fluctuations which might threaten the working or entrepreneurial classes. In an atmosphere of suspicion, violence and insecurity Hitler's propaganda played on emotion rather than reason; it satisfied a popular desire for certainty as against the intellectual difficulties posed by argument. Audiences came to Hitler to hear in the most uncompromising terms what they already wanted to believe – that their frustration and economic distress was entirely due to the revolution, the Republic and the betrayal of Germany's armed forces. Thus prepared, they were impressed by the unwavering ferocity of Nazi assaults on those who were supposed to have engineered Germany's downfall: the Marxists and the Jews.

When Hitler joined the DAP it had, like most other parties, a relatively democratic structure and was run by a committee. Most of the committee's members were old colleagues of Drexler, the Party Chairman. Hitler became dissatisfied with this leadership. His own army background and rhetorical gifts soon put him in a powerful position *vis-à-vis* his colleagues. He also disagreed with them on the issue of national organisation. They were interested in linking their movement with other racialist societies in Germany and Austria. Hitler rightly despised most of these groups as generals without armies, hoping to create an imposing façade behind which they had no substantial membership. He also realised that any amalgamation with another party would reduce his own status in Munich.

Matters came to a head in the summer of 1921. Hitler threatened to resign from the Party unless it was reorganised to give him dictatorial powers. The old committee was forced to capitulate. Hitler's local prestige had become so great that they dared not lose him. A three-man policy committee headed by Hitler was appointed to lead the Party. He also controlled an 'investigation' sub-committee, which regulated membership. Shortly after this the Nazis acquired a new business manager, the tough and efficient Max Amann. A former sergeant-major in Hitler's old regiment, Amann was completely loyal to him. With the neutralisation of the former party leadership, Hitler could rely on a more dependable local base than any other Völkisch politician in Germany. According to one report the Munich branch of the party alone could boast of 2500 paying registered members in the early months of 1921.[23]

Most of this progress can fairly be ascribed to Hitler, for it was his personality and contacts which drew into the party men who were prepared to devote time and sometimes money to the Nazi cause. Some of them were none too respectable in their private lives; many did not fit in socially with the high-minded artisans surrounding Drexler.

So far as funds were concerned, the party depended largely on the collections at meetings, individual gifts from wealthier sympathisers and membership dues. In all respects Hitler's contribution was vital. It was he who moved large audiences with his oratory, he who charmed bourgeois families like the Bechsteins, and he who attracted new membership in the provinces and in Munich itself. Even if others might wield more influence with potential donors, Hitler provided the fire in the movement which made it seem worth supporting. From 1921 to 1923 the party continued to make steady progress, recruiting members and opening new branches. Although it had organisations in northern Germany, its main support still came from Bavaria. By January 1922 there were six thousand registered party members, a very respectable figure for a Völkisch organisation.

In the summer of 1921 Hitler also organised his own strong-arm squads which, by 1923, had developed into a para-military force of some considerable size. This SA, as it was called, staged provocative demonstrations and was sometimes involved in street fights with opponents. Its chief function, however, was to prevent Nazi speakers being embarrassed by interruptions. Hitler never relished discussion; his forte was the monologue rather than the debate. In some ways this made his party more attractive to his audiences, for it stressed the contrast between Nazi ruthlessness and power and the apparent feebleness of their democratic opponents.

Although he owed his growing prestige to the loyalty of his Munich organisation, Hitler did not confine his activities to Bavaria. He travelled widely in Germany and other German-speaking regions to address meetings and contact sympathisers. He was by no means a provincially-minded politician when matters reached crisis point in 1923. The disaster which was to engulf Chancellor Cuno and destroy Germany's currency found Hitler prepared to exploit his first chance to make a bid for national power.

[1] The minister concerned was the Reich Finance Minister Dr Mayer, who became Ambassador in Paris.

[2] Brecht, *Aus nächster Nähe*, pp. 331–2.

[3] See Hitler's family tree in Bullock, *Hitler*, pp. 28–9. For an account of his possible Jewish connexion, Maser, *NSDAP*, pp. 46–8.

[4] See Cohn, *Warrant for Genocide*, pp. 108–17, 126 ff.

[5] See, for example, Kruck, *Alldeutscher Verband*. Also Pulzer, *Political Anti-Semitism*, pp. 190–1.

[6] Williams, 'Russians in Germany: 1900–1914', especially pp. 130–4.

[7] Bullock, *Hitler*, pp. 53–4; Maser, *NSDAP*, pp. 123–7.

[8] Maser, *NSDAP*, pp. 127–8.

[9] Ibid. pp. 45, 132.

[10] Deuerlein, '*Hitlers Eintritt in die Politik und die Reichswehr*'.

[11] Maser, *NSDAP*, pp. 150–1.

[12] Ibid. p. 167. Lists on which Hitler's name appears are at least partly in alphabetical order, and the numbers on the lists cannot therefore refer to the seniority of the members. In 1925, when the party was formally refounded, Hitler was given the number 1.

[13] See Phelps, 'Hitler als Parteiredner'.

[14] Bullock, *Hitler*, p. 66.

[15] Phelps, 'Hitler als Parteiredner', p. 287.

[16] Maser, *NSDAP*, pp. 472–4.

[17] *Handbuch des Alldeutschen Verbandes*, 1917.

[18] Phelps, 'Hitler als Parteiredner', p. 288.

[19] See, for example, Feder, *Der deutsche Staat*. On page 23 he writes: 'We National Socialists reject all forms of socialization or nationalization in the Marxist sense. Our economic ideal demands the greatest possible number of free enterprises, especially medium-size and small undertakings.'

[20] Rauschning, *Hitler Speaks*, p. 188.

[21] As given in Nolte, *Three Faces of Fascism*, p. 316. For the text of the letter in German see Deuerlein, 'Hitlers Eintritt in die NSDAP', p. 205.

[22] For a discussion of Hitler's power as a demagogue and its vital importance to the Nazi movement see Bullock, *Hitler*, pp. 68–73.

[23] Franz-Willing, *Hitlerbewegung*, p. 103. Also Maser, *NSDAP*, p. 264. For a discussion of Hitler's success in gaining control of the Nazi Party and the character of its organisation see Dietrich O. Orlow, 'The Organization and Structure of the NSDAP, 1919–1923' in *Journal of Modern History*, June 1965.

7 Ruhr Occupation and Inflation

CUNO's government was in no position to fight the French, but it refused to surrender to Poincaré's strong-arm tactics. Cuno inaugurated a policy of passive resistance in the Ruhr. Businessmen, officials and workers were not to co-operate with the occupying powers. The Reich government met the financial losses involved in this resistance. Acts of sabotage were also organised by clandestine para-military groups under the authority of the Reichswehr.[1] One result of these measures was that the Franco-Belgian invasion became a much larger operation than had been at first envisaged. Repressive measures were taken against recalcitrant German mine-owners, miners and civil servants. They included jail after courts martial and banishment from the occupied zone. Miners were shot down in clashes with French troops. A customs barrier was erected between the Ruhr area and the rest of the Reich.

This naturally represented an enormous financial and economic burden on the central government in Berlin. It was a burden that Cuno's régime was ill-fitted to bear. Germany's currency was in a desperate condition when Cuno assumed power. His defiance of the French only served to bury its slender chances of recovery. It should be emphasised that the inflation which had such a catastrophic and lasting effect on German society in the early 1920s cannot be blamed on the French occupation of the Ruhr.[2] By the time Poincaré moved his troops across the Rhine the Mark had already reached a stage of devaluation which rendered savings virtually worthless. At the beginning of 1920 the Mark had fallen to one-tenth of its pre-war value.

In the summer of 1922 it was worth only one-hundredth of the old mark, and by January 1923 one pre-war gold mark could have purchased 2500 paper-marks. This was, as Adolf Hitler's biographer has pointed out, a truly revolutionary development.[3] The socialist phrases used by Germany's first Republican administration had scarcely touched large sections of the population. The inflation, on the other hand, was like a plague, affecting all classes whatever their political persuasion or social status. Some of those who were in a position to speculate were able to make great financial gains. But many thousands more saw their security and living standards destroyed.

The inflation had begun during the war itself, but it had been assumed that peace would lead to stabilisation. The loss of the war, shortage of capital in German industry and the pressure of reparations demands prevented a halt being called in the inflationary process. The basic cause of this was a chronic deficit in the national budget. As we have seen, the German government initially took steps to remedy this by increasing taxation – especially direct taxation. But the value of money fell more rapidly than the tax estimates could anticipate. There remained a deficit which could only be met by printing more money. This encouraged the devaluation of the currency on world markets.

In the initial stages the inflation had had its advantages for the German economy. Cheap money meant that in-dustrial production could be reorganised quickly on a peace-time footing. New plant cost the industrialist little and wage bills were low in real terms. German export prices were lower than those of foreign competitors. Landowners could pay off mortgages more easily since their payments were in devalued currency. The government – always a heavy borrower – also benefited. The National Debt within Germany was virtually wiped out. Patriotic citizens who had invested in War Loans after 1914 saw their value dwindle into insignificance. Unwittingly they had made a present of their money to the State. They did not blame the Imperial government which had borrowed the money, but the Republican régime which had presided over its devaluation. The same catastrophe befell all those who had fixed interest savings. Deposit accounts, insurance policies, debenture stocks – in other words the staple investment areas for the cautious middle class – had all been undermined by the beginning of 1923.

However, it would be wrong to imagine that inflation harmed only the lower middle classes. Workers in the factories and the farms also found life very difficult in an inflationary situation. Cheap money certainly meant work – at least until the mark had ceased to have any value at all. But prices always raced ahead of wages. Hence, even though they were employed, the workers faced a steadily diminishing standard of living.

It was this situation which was grossly aggravated by Cuno's policy in the Ruhr. For now the downward plunge of the mark became so sharply aggravated that the figures ceased to have much meaning except to those speculators who were able to deal in foreign currency. Indeed, fixed prices were often abandoned and figures either referred to foreign currency or to the most recent quotations for the mark on foreign exchanges. Since bank depositors spent their money as soon as they received it the normal machinery of credit began to dry up and bank reserves were liquidated. Industrialists could no longer go on expanding production and unemployment began to add a new dimension to the misery of the working class.[4]

Cuno's policy of passive resistance to the French received vociferous support. But expressions of disgust at French action were not at all the same as declarations of loyalty towards the Republic. The extreme nationalists on the right and the Communists on the left did not give up their hostility to the government in Berlin simply because it was involved in a major crisis. Perhaps the most consistent opponent of the Republic was Adolf Hitler. He argued that Germany could never be strong while the Weimar system was allowed to continue. The Germans should therefore concentrate all their energies on destroying it. Only then could they hope to challenge France. He liked to call the politicians in Berlin 'November criminals', a reference to the November revolution of 1918. According to him, such people should be eliminated, and there could be no question of forming a 'common front' with them. Writing in the *Völkischer Beobachter*, he said:

So long as a nation does not do away with the assassins within its borders, no external successes can be possible. While written and spoken protests are directed against France, the real deadly enemy of the German people lurks within the walls of the nation. . . . Down with the November criminals, with all their nonsense about a united front![5]

The Communists' attitude was not so very different, although they did try to appeal to nationalist sentiment by attacks on Poincaré. They argued that Germany could only hope to liberate herself from Versailles by overthrowing capitalism and creating a proletarian dictatorship. The Ruhr crisis was denounced as a 'nationalist swindle'. On 23 January *Die Rote Fahne* carried the headline 'smite Poincaré and Cuno on the Ruhr and on the Spree'.*[6]

Such subversive tendencies were aggravated by the policies of Cuno's government. The complete collapse of the mark increased working-class bitterness and insecurity. The Communist Party – hitherto largely unsuccessful in its search for mass support – began to make perceptible gains in membership and voting strength.[7] On the right the Patriotic Leagues, with their para-military character, grew more powerful and belligerent, actively supported by the German army.[8]

French invasion of the Ruhr caused von Seeckt to intensify the recruitment and training of formations sometimes

* The Spree is the river on which Berlin stands.

referred to as the 'Black Reichswehr'. They stood in varying degrees of subordination to regular army officers. Generally speaking they received part-time training from the Reichswehr, for which some of them drew weapons from army depots. But many of the Patriotic Leagues – especially in Bavaria – had their own weapons in secret stock-piles. They were also careful not to put their members too directly under the army's control for fear of losing their political identity. This did not, however, prevent the Reichswehr chiefs from continuing to support them. Few army officers felt any more enthusiastic about the Republic than did the members of the Patriotic Leagues. General von Seeckt was concerned to maintain as effective discipline as possible among all Germany's forces – whether clandestine or otherwise – but he did not exert himself to ensure their loyalty to the Republic.

So long as Cuno remained in office pressure for a right-wing *coup* was unlikely to become very serious. But by the beginning of August it was clear that his ministry could not continue. Unable to cope with the economic and social problems facing Germany, Cuno resigned.

On 13 August Stresemann formed his first cabinet. He did so as the leader of a coalition in which all parties accepting the Republican Constitution were represented, from his own People's Party to the Social Democrats. Such broadly based support made it possible for him to envisage radical measures to overcome both the inflation and Germany's difficulties with the French. But he faced severe pressure from the nationalist opposition, supported as it was by powerful interests in agriculture, industry and the army. Von Seeckt himself had no very high opinion of Stresemann, and the presence of the Social Democrats in the Government outraged the Patriotic Leagues. On the other hand Stresemann's position was strengthened by a good grain harvest and by agreements between employers and trade unions to keep wages at least partly abreast of soaring prices.

Stresemann was ready to give up passive resistance in the Ruhr but sought concessions from Poincaré in return. None was forthcoming. German hopes that British pressure might cause the French to yield also proved vain. Although the British government disliked the occupation of the Ruhr it was not prepared to rupture relations with France for the sake of the Germans. When this was finally made clear to Stresemann he prepared for the unconditional cessation of passive resistance.[9]

This important change of policy was publicly announced on 26 September. At once there was swift reaction in Munich. Claiming that it faced a threat to internal order, the Bavarian cabinet declared a state of emergency and appointed Gustav von Kahr – who had resigned as Prime Minister in 1921 – as commissioner with dictatorial powers.[10] This move caused consternation in Berlin since it seemed to undermine the authority of the central government. Von Kahr was known as a determined opponent of the Republican régime. Stresemann's cabinet reacted by announcing a state of emergency throughout the Reich, and entrusting Defence Minister Gessler with emergency powers to maintain law and order. It soon became apparent, however, that the Bavarians would not accept orders from Berlin whatever the source of their authority.

Nor was disloyalty confined to Bavaria. In the early autumn of 1923 the German government faced numerous threats to its sovereignty. Some were overt, and took the form of localised rebellions. Potentially more serious was the clandestine network of intrigue aimed at deposing the parliamentary régime in Berlin itself. Participants in such machinations included leaders of the Patriotic Leagues, nationalist politicians in both the National People's Party and the German People's Party, industrialists and army leaders.

The atmosphere in the Reichswehr was particularly disturbing from a Republican viewpoint. Since the previous

January the army had been preparing for a possible war
with France and had completely ignored the restrictions
placed upon it by the Versailles Peace Treaty. The end of
passive resistance was seen as yet another Republican capitu-
lation to the enemy. In the words of one lieutenant-colonel it
was 'a new lost war'. He remarked bitterly that the army now
had two duties: 'protection of the constitution, of a diseased
system, and preparation of the war of liberation, which
is prevented by the system . . .'.[11] This was a gross distortion
of the facts, but it was a widely-held view in military circles.

The first open symptom of revolt came at the beginning
of October when units of the 'Black Reichswehr' mutinied in
Kustrin and Spandau – uncomfortably near Berlin. Led by
a former participant in the Kapp Putsch called Major
Buchrucker, the dissidents were quickly overpowered by
regular Reichswehr units. Von Seeckt himself had no
sympathy for undisciplined soldiery of the freebooting
Freikorps type who formed the backbone of the clandestine
military formations recruited during 1923. But no severe
measures were taken against the mutineers. Buchrucker
received a term of 'honourable imprisonment'.[12]

The Reichswehr was more enthusiastic when suppressing
Communist subversion which was threatening in central
Germany. The German Communist Party was at last
preparing to embark on a new wave of revolutionary
activity. It was being encouraged by the international
Communist organisation, the Comintern. Partly as a result
of domestic power struggles in Moscow the Russian
Communist leadership had decided that the time was ripe
for their German comrades to seize power. Russian political
and military specialists were sent to Germany to help
organise the fight. Funds were collected in Russia to aid the
German proletariat in its forthcoming struggle.[13] The
leader of the German Communist Party, Brandler, was
aware that his party was in no condition to launch such a
dangerous adventure, but in face of his ebullient and

experienced Russian comrades he quelled his doubts. The Communist effort was to be concentrated in the two central German states of Saxony and Thuringia, where the Land governments were headed by left-wing Social Democrats. It was hoped to use these states as a proletarian power base from which revolution would spread over Germany. The government in Berlin acted too quickly for the Comintern's plan to be put into effect. Using its emergency powers, it appointed Reich Commissioners in both states and deposed their Prime Ministers. These measures were effected by the Reichswehr, which enthusiastically overawed opposition by a show of armed force. The KPD had suffered another humiliating reverse.

Such strong measures against the danger of left-wing subversion brought demands from the Social Democratic members of Stresemann's cabinet that action should be taken to quell the far more dangerous mutineers in Bavaria. Ever since the appointment of von Kahr as State Commissioner in Munich the extent of Bavarian insubordination had been growing more obvious.

The commander of the Bavarian section of the Reichswehr, Lieutenant-General von Lossow, refused to obey instructions from the Reichswehr Ministry and looked to von Kahr for authority. Von Kahr himself was hoping for political changes in Berlin. Neither he nor von Lossow was a Bavarian separatist. They wanted an eventual restoration of the Wittelsbach monarchy in Bavaria, but envisaged this as being within the framework of the German Reich.

On 22 October the Bavarian Reichswehr took an oath of loyalty to von Kahr's government. Two days later von Lossow explained Bavarian policy to a gathering of staff officers, state officials and para-military leaders. The Government's purpose, he said, was to establish a new régime in Berlin—evidently by force. This would have to take place within three weeks, but in the meantime he urged the Patriotic Leagues to exercise discipline and restraint.[14]

The Bavarians were pinning their hopes on Nationalist groups in Berlin – and in particular on action by the head of the Reichswehr, General von Seeckt. Von Seeckt did indeed make efforts to overthrow Stresemann. He complained to Ebert that the army no longer had confidence in the Chancellor, and, when this had no effect, leaked news of his displeasure to some of Stresemann's rivals in the People's Party. Stresemann's position was shaken, but he remained in office. Von Seeckt was too cautious to do more, and the Bavarians were warned to avoid precipitate action.

Restraint was possible for von Kahr and von Lossow, but not for Hitler. He had been made leader of a union of para-military formations in Bavaria – the so-called *Kampfbund*. This included the most radical and impatient of the Nationalist Leagues. Hitler distrusted the official Bavarian leadership and its conservative allies in northern Germany. He rightly suspected that they were more concerned with restoring the ascendency of the old ruling classes than with regenerating Germany along Völkisch lines. He realised that von Lossow wanted to use the Kampfbund to further his own plans, but would not give Hitler any very responsible part to play in the political developments which were expected to follow. The same suspicious attitude prevailed in the breast of General Ludendorff, whose great prestige was now attached to the Völkisch wing of the nationalist movement in Bavaria.

Hitler decided he must take matters into his own hands. On the night of 8 November his SA men burst in upon a meeting at the Bürgerbräukeller in Munich, where von Kahr was holding forth to a large and distinguished audience on the moral justification for dictatorship. By a mixture of bluff and threats Hitler persuaded von Kahr, von Lossow and Ludendorff to join him in establishing a new national government.

There is still some doubt about the motives of von Kahr and von Lossow at this moment. After the *coup* had failed they naturally claimed to have been acting under duress and to have deceived Hitler with their promises to support him. Actually it seems quite likely that they were carried away by the enthusiasm of their Beer Hall audience and the authority of General Ludendorff. One of those present later compared the emotional scenes in the Bürgerbräukeller with the Rütli oath in Schiller's *Wilhelm Tell*.[15] To von Kahr and von Lossow the differences between Hitler's objectives and their own were not very great in the short term – both wanted to overthrow the Berlin government. Hitler could always be restrained when the action was over. It was a dangerous mode of thought which was to reappear later with more tragic results.

The Putsch in Munich was short-lived. Its suppression was mainly due to the hostile attitude adopted by von Lossow's immediate subordinates in the Bavarian Reichswehr. The commander of the Munich garrison took steps to ensure that army units remained loyal to their officers, and that weapons were not distributed to Hitler's supporters. The State Police were ordered to secure communications centres. Von Lossow had to reverse these actions or disown Hitler. He chose the latter course. In the early hours of the morning von Kahr and von Lossow issued a statement condemning the Putsch.

On 9 November Hitler – encouraged by Ludendorff – made a last desperate bid for support by marching his paramilitary formations into the centre of Munich. The march was more of a demonstration than a military operation. Ludendorff and Hitler gambled on the reluctance of police and troops to fire on them. These were tactics similar to those used by Eisner's revolutionaries five years earlier.

At first they seemed to be succeeding; police cordons melted away and the crowds in the streets were friendly. But when the procession neared the centre of the city it passed through a narrow street leading past the former royal palace. There a more resolute detachment of Bavarian State

Police barred the way. An exchange of fire took place. Hitler's neighbour in the march was mortally wounded and pulled Hitler to the ground as he fell. Others in the procession fell flat or scattered. Within minutes the demonstrators had fled and the Putsch was over.

The failure of the Putsch meant that the Republic was secure from internal subversion for several years to come. Indeed, Hitler drew the lesson that state power could only be achieved from within. Putsches were unlikely to succeed. The state of emergency was maintained throughout Germany for four months. It was administered by von Seeckt with perfect correctness. Although the Social Democrats still refused to support Stresemann as Chancellor and he was forced to resign on 23 November, a new coalition under the Centre Party leader, Wilhelm Marx, included him as Foreign Minister, a post he held until his death in 1929. He was thereby in a position to carry on the patient work of extricating Germany from her desperate international position.

The ability of Republican governments to withstand conspiratorial assaults increased the tendency among the monarchist and authoritarian opponents of the régime to make compromises with it. A year later German Nationalist ministers entered a Republican government. But popular faith in the Republican system – never very strong – had been badly, and in some cases permanently, shaken by the events of 1923. The collapse of the currency left behind it a legacy of resentment, especially among Germany's numerous lower middle class. When the time came, Hitler was to be the beneficiary.

1 Carsten, *Reichswehr*, pp. 154–5.
2 Heiber, *Die Republik von Weimar*, pp. 97–100.
3 Bullock, *Hitler*, p. 91.

[4] See the figures for the percentage of unemployed Trade Unionists given in Appendix III, 4 of Angell, *The Recovery of Germany*, pp. 370–1. This shows 0·6 per cent unemployed in June 1922 as against 4·2 per cent in June 1923. June was the second best month in 1923.

[5] Bullock, *Hitler*, pp. 91–2.

[6] Angress, *Stillborn Revolution*, p. 295.

[7] Ibid., pp. 359–61. Angress points out that such gains were probably not as great as some enthusiastic writers have suggested.

[8] For a good discussion of the Bavarian Patriotic Leagues see Hofmann, *Der Hitlerputsch*, pp. 59–65.

[9] Turner, *Stresemann*, p. 117.

[10] Hofmann, *Hitlerputsch*, pp. 94–9. See also Deuerlein, *Hitlerputsch*, pp. 180–2. For Bavarian views on Stresemann's cabinet see ibid. pp. 159–61.

[11] Carsten, *Reichswehr*, p. 164.

[12] Ibid. p. 168. Also Gordon, *Reichswehr*, pp. 233–4.

[13] Angress, *Stillborn Revolution*, pp. 395–7. Also ibid. pp. 418–19.

[14] Deuerlein, *Hitlerputsch*, pp. 257–8.

[15] Hofmann, *Hitlerputsch*, p. 168; the observer was Professor Karl Alexander von Müller. For accounts of the events in the Bürgerbräu-keller see Bullock, *Hitler*, pp. 106–9; Hofmann, op. cit. pp. 150–69. Kahr's own account of the Putsch, which – although confidential – was designed to be seen by too many officials to guarantee absolute frankness, is printed in Deuerlein, *Hitlerputsch*, pp. 495–8.

8 Towards Recovery

HAVING survived foreign occupation and internal sub-version from the right and left, the Republic found its situation improving. Three important achievements marked the post-crisis era. The first, which had already been embarked upon when Hitler launched his abortive *coup*, was the stabilisation of the currency. The second was the Dawes Agreement, regulating Germany's reparations payments, and the third was the Locarno Treaty.

By the autumn of 1923 a new currency had become essential to Germany if serious unrest was to be avoided during the winter. For some time various schemes had been canvassed to overcome the problem. The government had to be particularly careful not to upset agricultural interests by its remedial measures, for if the farmers were dissatisfied food supplies might suffer.[1] Hans Luther, the Food Minister, was especially insistent that urgent steps be taken to end the inflation. Largely as the result of his prompting, the Government accepted a scheme whereby a new currency should be based on land and industrial values. A loan was to be issued to the Reichsbank from a specially constituted authority, the Rentenbank. The loan was backed by a mortgage, first of all on agricultural property and then on industrial resources. The Reichsbank could issue Renten-marks to the value of its loan holding. Rentenmarks were valued at one gold mark each. The old paper-marks were to be gradually redeemed at their current value. The agrarian backing for the new currency was, of course, largely fictitious, because land is not convertible in the same way as gold. Nevertheless, since Germany lacked enough gold to launch a new bullion-backed currency, the psychological effect of the Rentenmark's paper mortgage helped to maintain its value. The restricted amount of the new currency available to the Reichsbank also prevented a slide towards inflation. Most important of all was the fact that the Government could no longer draw on unlimited currency credits from the Reichsbank but had to try to balance expenditure against income.

The introduction of the new currency involved many problems and hardships. That the Rentenmark succeeded at all was largely due to the energy of Luther, who became Finance Minister at the beginning of October. Luther gave decisive support to the Rentenmark scheme and once it was under way prevented the pleas of vested interests from undermining it. He appointed a Currency Commissioner, Hjalmar Schacht, to deal with problems arising from the introduction of the new mark. The firmness of both men contributed to the success of revaluation. The following summer the Rentenmark was replaced by the Reichsmark, which was to remain the German unit of currency until after the Second World War.

The stabilisation programme in Germany meant that economic life revived throughout the Reich, although dearer money caused a high level of unemployment. Fears that the Rentenmark would soon begin to be devalued proved groundless. On the other hand, the French began to experience financial troubles, and the franc came under heavy pressure. Elections were held for the French Chamber and in May Poincaré was defeated. The new Prime Minister, Édouard Herriot, was more interested in conciliation than extortion. The threat to German integrity in the West ebbed away. Instead there appeared a real chance of tackling the Republic's international and financial problems by negotiation and compromise.

It was in this more favourable atmosphere that the discussion over the Dawes Plan took place. The work of an inter-Allied Committee chaired by two Americans, Charles

E

Dawes and Owen D. Young, it approached the problem of German financial stability from a self-consciously business-like standpoint. Wherever possible, political pitfalls were avoided. Nevertheless, the report had enormous political implications. Its major concern was to establish a scale of reparations payments which would not prevent Germany from stabilising her currency and balancing her budget.

On 9 April 1924 the committee submitted its recommendations. They were undoubtedly more practicable than any previously produced by a similar body. They involved firm guarantees that the Germans would make regular annual payments, a controlled system of transfer which would protect Germany's currency from threats of devaluation, and a loan from the Western Powers to help Germany start payments and initiate an economic recovery. If there was a weakness in the scheme it lay in the firm economic optimism with which Dawes and his colleagues regarded the future. Speaking of the potentialities of Germany, Dawes wrote:

The task would be hopeless if the present situation of Germany accurately reflected her potential capacity; the proceeds from Germany's national production could not in that case enable her to meet the national needs and to ensure the payment of her foreign debts.

But Germany's growing and industrious population; her great technical skill; the wealth of her material resources; the development of her agriculture along progressive lines; her eminence in industrial science; all these factors enable us to be hopeful with regard to her future production.

After referring to the large-scale renewal of plant which had taken place in Germany after the war Dawes continued:

Germany is therefore well equipped with resources; she possesses the means for exploiting them on a large scale; when the present credit shortage has been overcome, she will be able to resume a favoured position in the activity of a world where normal conditions of exchange are restored.[2]

The success of the Dawes reparations scheme therefore required a prosperous Germany. Indeed, the report envisaged a continuous growth in Germany's economic strength and made arrangements that future prosperity should benefit reparations creditors as well as the Germans themselves. In one sense the committee's reasoning was quite correct; Germany undoubtedly had the physical capacity to increase production. It might perhaps have been asked whether the development of world trade would allow her to utilise this capacity. Dawes and his colleagues were not required to face that question, nor could they have been expected to provide a realistic answer.

The Dawes scheme was criticised in Germany because it involved submitting to Allied controls over the central banking system and the railways. These would be supervised by committees consisting of German and Allied representatives. The railways were to be run for profits, part of which would go to repay a loan raised for reparations. The central bank's credit policy was to be controlled to ensure currency stability. The German government was to pledge certain revenues for the repayment of its debts, and German industry, which the Dawes Committee judged to have profited from inflation, was to bear a special debt of five thousand million marks for the benefit of Germany's reparations creditors.[3] These provisions were seen as a monstrous invasion of German sovereignty.

The German Nationalist Party campaigned against the Plan as a 'second Versailles'. But influential pressure groups within the party – agricultural and business interests and even the leaders of the Reichswehr – saw that the Plan would bring Germany great material advantages. In a crucial vote in the Reichstag on 28 August 1924 the Nationalists split on this issue and some of them voted for the implementation of the Plan, which was duly carried into effect.

By the beginning of 1925 the Nationalists were themselves represented in the cabinet – under the Chancellorship of

Luther. They soon found a new target for their patriotic indignation.

The cause of their displeasure was a security pact which Stresemann was attempting to negotiate with Germany's western neighbours. This would involve a recognition of German frontiers in the West and membership of the League of Nations. The Nationalists regarded such moves as tantamount to treason. They had refused to accept the final loss of Alsace-Lorraine and demanded that the Allies must renounce what they described as the 'war-guilt lie'. As for the League of Nations, this had been bitterly unpopular in Germany ever since she had been kept out of it in 1919.

It was also feared that German relations with the Soviet Union would be damaged by entry into the League. The Russians regarded it with even more hostility than did the Germans. They feared German participation in League sanctions against Russia. The Reichswehr set its face firmly against any move which might weaken its ties with the Red Army. Stresemann managed to overcome all this opposition to his policy. To do so he relied on guile and diplomacy.

The Russians were mollified, if not entirely consoled, with a trade pact favourable to the Soviet Union and a successful German effort to interpret the Article on sanctions in the League Charter so that it was, in the words of the Russian Foreign Minister, Chicherin, 'really emasculated'.[4] The Nationalists were persuaded to stay in the German cabinet for domestic reasons – not the least of which was their desire to affect tariff policy – and by the hope that when any agreement was made public the blame for its shortcomings could be heaped on Stresemann, who would then have to resign. But Chancellor Luther, after a moment of doubtful loyalty to his Foreign Minister, decided to associate himself formally with Stresemann's policy and the Nationalist plan proved unsuccessful.[5] A conference was convened in the Swiss town of Locarno to negotiate the Western security pact.

For Luther and Stresemann it was a considerable diplomatic success. The nationalist pressures within his own country enabled Stresemann to reject French and British proposals which were unattractive to him. Hence he was able to obtain Anglo-French agreement for the interpretation of Article 16 of the League Charter in a sense which would absolve Germany from the responsibility to participate in joint action – whether economic, financial or military – against an aggressor. He was able to restrict the frontier guarantees contained in the final agreements to Germany's western boundaries with France and Belgium; the eastern frontiers were not accepted by Germany as final. He was able to restrict the most important negotiations to a charmed circle of Western nations from which France's allies in Eastern Europe – in particular the Czechs and the Poles – were excluded. This was to foreshadow events in the 1930s when the concept of a four-power consortium to settle European problems – the powers in question being Britain, France, Italy and Germany – culminated in the notorious betrayal of Czechoslovakia at Munich in September 1938. Stresemann himself expressed his satisfaction about this discomfiture of Germany's eastern neighbours when he told a delighted audience in Berlin:

Messrs Beneš and Skrzynski* had to sit there in an adjoining room until we allowed them to come in. That was the position of states which had previously been so inflated in importance because they were the servants of others, and which were dropped the moment it seemed possible to make an agreement with Germany.[6]

The Locarno Agreements took the form of a Western non-aggression pact between France, Belgium and

* Beneš and Skrzynski were the Czechoslovakian and Polish representatives at Locarno. They were not allowed to participate in the major discussions. Beneš was the President of Czechoslovakia in 1938.

Germany, guaranteed by Italy and Great Britain. Arbitration agreements were signed between Germany and France and Belgium to ensure the peaceful settlement of future disputes. Germany concluded similar arbitration arrangements with Poland and Czechoslovakia. She did not, however, accept the finality of her frontiers with those countries. Stresemann claimed that legal opinion on the arbitration treaties held that Germany need feel no restriction on resorting to war in the East if the occasion arose.[7]

Stresemann's own motives in concluding the treaties have been the subject of much speculation – a good deal of it superfluous. Stresemann naturally presented himself to his diplomatic colleagues in the West as the champion of European *rapprochement*. The negotiations which culminated in the Locarno Treaties generated a good many public statements at international gatherings stressing the need for a new era of peaceful co-operation. In 1926 Stresemann himself was to be awarded the Nobel Peace Prize. After his death sections of his diaries and papers were published, and it was hardly surprising that the editors selected those which reinforced the picture of Stresemann the peacemaker, Stresemann the good European. With German defeat in the Second World War a great deal more documentary evidence became available – much of it in the files of the German Foreign Office. It became clear that, at the time when he was working for a *détente* in the West, Stresemann was also expressing strongly nationalist points of view over such questions as the future of Germany's eastern frontiers and the possible union with Austria. In addition, there could no longer be any doubt that he knew of the secret military arrangements between Berlin and Moscow.[8]

There was nothing particularly surprising in these revelations. The real difference lay in the climate of opinion before and after the Second World War. Stresemann had always been a German nationalist in the sense that he wanted to further German interests in the diplomatic

sphere. His career in the war and after it had demonstrated this. He made few bones about the fact that it
was German weakness, not a belief in pacific courses for
their own sake, which forced him to make concessions over
such matters as passive resistance in the Ruhr, reparations
or the recognition of Germany's western frontier.

So far as Locarno was concerned Stresemann believed
that it would forestall a bilateral Anglo-French treaty,
hasten the removal of Allied troops from the Rhineland, and
create an atmosphere of *détente* in which Germany could
rebuild her economic strength. By keeping a free hand in the
east and maintaining his Russian connexion, he could still
hope for territorial adjustments *vis-à-vis* Poland. This does
not mean that he was hypocritical in his attitude towards
the Western Powers. It is unlikely that French or British
statesmen really imagined that Stresemann, formerly of the
Pan-German League, had been transformed into a fervent
internationalist. They knew the German Foreign Minister
as a tough negotiator who was well able to defend the
interests of his country.

The fact was that the British and the French governments
were willing to accept a *modus vivendi* with Germany, even if
it did give the Reich a more favourable position than it had
possessed since 1918. The cost of repressing Germany was
high. Collaboration between the four Western Powers –
France, Britain, Germany and Italy – might bring economic benefits to all. As for secret rearmament, Western
observers were well aware that Germany had not fulfilled
the Versailles disarmament clauses. They realised also that
the extent of Germany's illegal rearmament could not pose
a real military threat to her neighbours. Throughout the
Weimar period the German army was hardly strong enough
to fight the Poles, let alone wage war on France. Stresemann
himself was ready to allow an increase in military power so
long as the Reichswehr did not thereby jeopardise his own
diplomatic manoeuvres. Despite friction with von Seeckt

and his colleagues, the Foreign Ministry was never baulked of its objectives by military obstruction.

As for the League of Nations, Stresemann regarded this with no more enthusiasm than most of his countrymen. But he realised that Germany would be better able to defend her international interests from within the League than if she stayed outside it. When she was finally admitted to League membership in the autumn of 1926 he used this new platform at Geneva* to air the grievances of German minorities under foreign rule – particularly those in Poland.

The Germans had also harboured hopes that the League might be persuaded to consider more general questions affecting Germany and her former enemies. The first of these was disarmament, over which Germany demanded equality. The Western Powers must either disarm down to her level or let her rearm up to theirs. Although the League devoted itself with great assiduity to the problem of disarmament, no solution was ever found. On the surface the issue was technical; it was impossible to find a proper balance between powers of different sizes and geographical situations. Basically it was political – no German government was satisfied with Germany's restricted condition, and no French government was prepared to see the more numerous Germans achieve military equality with France.

Lastly, the German hope that Allied troop withdrawals would be more rapid after the Locarno agreements was only partly fulfilled. Although the Cologne Zone was evacuated and the Allied military control commission for the supervision of German rearmament ceased to function, Allied troops remained in the Rhineland. It was not until the summer of 1929 that their withdrawal was finally promised to the Germans, and by then the 'spirit of Locarno' was ebbing rapidly away.

German public opinion was not therefore immediately impressed with Locarno. There was a basic divergence

* The headquarters of the League.

between the German and the Anglo-French attitudes
towards it. In London and Paris it was seen as the termination of a war-like period; the final establishment of European
stability. Austen Chamberlain, the British Foreign Secretary,
described it as 'the real dividing line between the years of
war and the years of peace'.[9]

To the Germans it was only the beginning of an era
which would see the dismantling of the whole Versailles
Treaty. This does not mean that the diplomats and Republican politicians in Berlin were preparing a new world
war. It does not mean that Stresemann was a Nazi in striped
trousers and a frock-coat. But it did mean that many
Germans had still to face up to the realities of the post-war
world. When these realities were compounded by a sudden
economic crisis they fled into even wilder realms of fantasy
conjured up for them by Adolf Hitler.

On the domestic front these were gloomy years for the
parties of the Weimar coalition. Currency stabilisation and
the Dawes Plan were not vote-catching achievements.
Germany was still in the grip of economic hardship and
national humiliation. Those bearing responsibility for the
nation's affairs suffered for it politically.

The German Nationalists reaped the rewards of opposition by making substantial gains in Reichstag elections held
in May 1924. The Social Democrats – who had actually left
the Government in November 1923, but who were associated
with Republican policies – lost ground. They found themselves facing a serious rival in the competition for working-
class allegiance. This was the German Communist Party,
which collected three-and-a-half million votes – well over
half the number given to the SPD. Henceforward the KPD
was to be a dangerous magnet for working-class militants.
It was especially attractive to the young. Its leadership
presented a far more youthful and dynamic image than the
ageing bureaucracy of the SPD.

Of the moderate parties, the Democrats and Stresemann's

People's Party had also fared very badly at the polls. But their defeat did not induce them to close ranks against extremism. Koch-Weser, the leader of the Democrats, did initiate proposals for a merger with Stresemann's People's Party, but was rebuffed. The DVP was more inclined to seek an arrangement with the German Nationalists, and in any case Stresemann had not forgotten his treatment at the hands of the Democrats in the early days of the Republic. Hopes of a united liberal party opposed to socialism but loyal to the Republic were once again torpedoed.

New Reichstag elections in December 1924 scarcely changed the situation. In February the following year the Republican parties received another blow when Friedrich Ebert died. The presidential election which followed – the first popular vote for this office – brought success to Field-Marshal Paul von Hindenburg, the hero of Kaiser Wilhelm's army and an important contributor to the 'stab-in-the-back' theory.

Hindenburg's victory was not foreseen when the election campaign began. Initially he was not even a candidate. Yet in the first round of voting none of the orthodox party politicians managed to win an overall majority. The SPD and the Democrats decided to unite their forces behind the candidate of the Centre, Wilhelm Marx. The right-wing parties felt that only a man with genu-inely national appeal could defeat Marx, and they plumped for Hindenburg. Stresemann himself was dismayed by this decision, since he thought that it would outrage foreign opinion. Had he pressed his objections Hindenburg might have withdrawn, but instead the Foreign Minister chose to remain silent.

The Field-Marshal defeated Marx by a narrow margin. His cause was aided by the Communists, who persisted in running their own candidate despite the displeasure of the Comintern in Moscow. Nearly two million votes were wasted on their man, although it is not certain that they would otherwise have gone to Marx. It was also evident that there had been defections from the Democrats and Centre Party in favour of Hindenburg.[10]

The result was not helpful for the Republic in the long run, although its immediate effects did not seem very dramatic. The Field-Marshal was greeted on his arrival in Berlin by crowds of admirers waving black, white and red flags – the colours of the old Empire. Stresemann was shocked to find Hindenburg reading the reactionary *Kreuzzeitung** when he made his first official visit to the President. But the Foreign Minister had nothing to complain of in the way business was conducted. A flurry of outraged foreign press comment – particularly in Paris – subsided when it was seen that Hindenburg's assumption of power was not accompanied by any sinister changes in German policy. Superficially his election implied a strengthening of state authority, since the Presidency was now no longer an object of anti-Republican revilement except from the Nazis and the Communists.

Hindenburg's election can be seen as an attempt by the German people to flee from the responsibilities of parliamentary government back to the comforting safety of pre-war authority. Hindenburg represented order and security; commodities which the Republic had been unable to provide. The Field-Marshal was an old man unendowed with political talent. He was aptly described by his English biographer as 'The Wooden Titan'.[11] He accepted the Weimar Constitution and did not consciously set out to betray it. He was a great disappointment to those who had hoped to use him as a stalking horse for a monarchist restoration or some other form of dictatorship.

Yet Hindenburg never identified himself whole-heartedly with the Republic. He still felt bound by ties of loyalty to the Emperor Wilhelm II, whose irresponsible arrogance

* Traditionally the newspaper of the German conservatives, especially the East Elbean landowners.

had not been diminished by his exile in Holland. The President tolerated many violently anti-Republican figures among his personal circle of friends, and although he resisted their more obviously subversive suggestions, their influence depressed and confused him. Had he possessed a more forceful personality he might have been able to win many of the more reasonable conservative elements over to positive collaboration with the new régime. As it was, his influence was largely negative; he refused to betray the Republic, but he did not rally the people to its banner.

This is not to suggest that popular support for the Republic was nowhere to be found. One of the most striking developments on the domestic scene in 1924 was the birth of a new Republican defence organisation, the *Reichsbanner Schwarz-Rot-Gold*. Despite the reluctance shown by Social Democratic leaders to encourage militant self-help among their own followers, the turbulent events of 1923 had provoked an active response among those who wished to protect German democracy.

The provincial governor of Magdeburg, a tough Social Democrat called Otto Hirsing, decided to establish a para-military force open to all those willing to demonstrate their loyalty in action. The Reichsbanner, as it was called, quickly mushroomed to success. Social Democratic Party locals formed the basis for its growth, but non-Socialists were also encouraged to join. Within a year the Reichsbanner could claim over a million members, and had become the most successful para-military formation in Germany. Its demonstrations and propaganda reached the remotest parts of the country, teaching the population to celebrate the foundation of their new Republic, honour its flag and its constitution. The Reichsbanner proved that Republicans could don uniforms, march in step and prepare to fight for their beliefs with as much enthusiasm as any Nationalist rivals.[12]

By the end of 1925 such enthusiasm did not seem misplaced. As the German economy began to revive under the impact of the Dawes Plan and as the country's international position showed obvious signs of improvement, it seemed that the Weimar Republic might be able to establish itself on a firmer foundation than had been possible in the difficult years after the revolution.

[1] Schacht, *Stabilization of the Mark*. Also Luther, *Politiker ohne Partei*, pp. 156–68.

[2] 'Reports of the Expert Committees appointed by the Reparations Commission. English Version', Cmd 2105, 1924 (London HMSO, 1924) pp. 14–15, in *State Papers*, 1924, vol. xxvii, pp. 844 ff.

[3] Bergmann, *Reparationen*, pp. 285–9.

[4] For a good account of the Russian opposition to Locarno see Freund, *Unholy Alliance*, pp. 213–44.

[5] Turner, *Stresemann*, pp. 204–8, 217.

[6] Stresemann's speech to the 'Landesmannschaften in Gross-Berlin', 14 December 1925. *Akten zur deutschen auswärtigen Politik*, series B, vol. II, p. 752. Stresemann's account was exaggerated. The Czechs and the Poles signed the final protocol of the conference and were reassured by defensive agreements with France.

[7] Cf. Stresemann's speech to the Landesmannschaften, 14 December 1925. See note 6. This interpretation was a very sophisticated one and did not accord with the spirit of the agreements or the wording of the preamble. But Stresemann himself was presenting the treaties to a nationalistically minded audience, and there is no reason to suppose he was particularly concerned about the military issue. On the other hand, he had been very careful not to commit Germany to an 'Eastern Locarno'. This latter possibility was most distasteful to the German Foreign Office, which consistently resisted any suggestion of a *detente* in the East.
The terms of the Locarno Agreements are given in *Survey of International Affairs 1925*, vol. II, by C. A. Macartney and others, pp. 439–52.

[8] See Stresemann, *Vermächtnis*; Gatzke, *Stresemann*, and 'The Stresemann Papers'; Thimme, *Stresemann*. For a good illustration of Stresemann's awareness of the Russo-German arms collaboration see his letter to Gessler enclosing a report on a conversation about this between Trotsky and Brockdorff-Rantzau in June 1924, printed in Freund, *Unholy Alliance*, pp. 254–8.

[9] Quoted in *Survey of International Affairs 1925*, vol. II, by Macartney and others, p. 56.

[10] On the Hindenburg election see Dorpalen, *Hindenburg*, pp. 64–89; Turner, *Stresemann*, pp. 191–202.

[11] Wheeler-Bennett, *Hindenburg*.

[12] For an important study of the Reichsbanner see Rohe, *Reichsbanner*.

9 The Semblance of Stability: 1924–1929

In the three years which followed the Locarno Agreements Germany enjoyed internal peace and a stable relationship with foreign powers. Republican politicians were no longer under a constant threat of assassination. The number of right-wing para-military formations dwindled. The army began to show itself more amenable to civilian control. Even the German Nationalist Party, seeing no future in sterile opposition, tacitly compromised its monarchist principles in the quest for political power.

In foreign affairs the Germans achieved a modest success in the summer of 1927 when the Allies agreed to a reduction of 10,000 in their Rhineland occupation forces. At home the Reichstag managed to agree to a generous unemployment insurance law. This was a major piece of social legislation, even though it could only be self-financing if unemployment were stabilised at a relatively low level. That did not seem an unreal hope. By 1927 German production exceeded that of 1913. Foreign trade was larger in volume than before the war, although Germany's share of world markets had fallen and her import/export balance was unfavourable. Looking back on the grim situation in 1923 it seemed that Germany had experienced a remarkable economic recovery.

Superficially at least, the Republic had been granted a period of economic, political and diplomatic stability. How far had it managed to consolidate itself? In terms of electoral success there seemed real grounds for optimism. General elections held in May 1928 brought a clear victory for those parties which accepted the constitution. Extremists on the right and left gained less than 30 per cent of the votes cast. This figure included the supporters of the German Nationalist Party, which had participated in Republican cabinets and accepted – albeit with bad grace – the main lines of Stresemann's foreign policy in the post-Locarno period. The Nationalists lost thirty seats in the 1928 elections and the Social Democrats gained twenty-two. Socialist ministers entered the cabinet for the first time since 1923, and one of their number, Hermann Müller, became Reich Chancellor. President Hindenburg seemed quite willing to work loyally with the Social Democrats in his government. Indeed, he had a high opinion of Müller and compared him favourably with other Chancellors.[1]

Despite these signs of political improvement, the Republic had been unable to root itself very firmly in German society. Perhaps it was asking too much to expect it to do so in such a short space of time.

Economically the country still faced very serious problems. Its industrial and financial recovery had been deceptive in its rapidity. Although Germany seemed prosperous, the manner of achieving success had not been that envisaged by the authors of the Dawes Plan. They had intended that the German reparations burden should be sustained by a domestic tax surplus and by a favourable import/export balance. Hence Germany should really pay her way both at home and abroad. Neither of these conditions was met. Germany's trade figures always showed imports outrunning exports, while the national budget did not produce the sort of surpluses that had been hoped for. Indeed during the years 1924–30 there was an overall deficit of nearly 1300 million Reichsmarks.[2] Hence the reparations payments made by Germany were really being financed by foreign loans. In addition, the capital needs of German industry could not find satisfaction in domestic profits or savings. Germany was still suffering from the loss of capital which had taken place during the wild post-war inflation. German industrialists were eager to re-equip their factories with new plant, but many of the funds for such enterprises had to be borrowed from abroad. The result was an unhealthy dependence on foreign capital for economic prosperity.

The Dawes scheme itself was to some extent responsible for this state of affairs. It had imposed restrictions on the German money designed to prevent a repetition of Germany's inflation. The country's own financial leaders were also eager to prevent the Mark slipping again. The Reichsbank was prevented by the Dawes legislation from allowing its interest rate to drop below 5 per cent. On the other hand it had no effective power to stop private banks from lending money or borrowing it from abroad.[3] German interest rates were therefore kept high, and the country became very attractive to overseas investors. They could achieve as good or even better returns on capital lent on a short-term basis to Germany, than they could from longer-term investments in their own countries. As a result, German indebtedness to foreigners rose sharply. The country even enjoyed a favourable balance of payments because of the loan funds pouring into it. But well over half of this debt was in the form of loans which could quickly be recalled if investors lost confidence in the Republic's economic prospects.[4]

If the Republic was economically vulnerable it had yet to develop institutions upon which it could rely unconditionally in times of crisis. The Reichswehr was a case in point. In the years 1924–8 the army certainly showed a greater willingness to collaborate with Republican politicians. Von Seeckt resigned in October 1926, and his successor General Heye was a less forceful officer. He even admitted that the army had been sometimes at fault in its relations with civilian authorities – something which would have been quite unthinkable during von Seeckt's period of office.[5]

The Reichswehr made genuine efforts to improve its relations with Republican parties in the Reichstag. The Reichswehr regularised some of its clandestine payments for purposes forbidden under the Versailles Treaty. Its official budget rose by roughly 75 per cent between 1924 and 1928. Some apparently harmless items of expenditure were inflated and the surplus put to other uses. In addition, money was secretly made over to the army from other ministerial budgets, including the Reich Ministry of Transport. Previously funds set aside for confidential purposes had been known only to the army officers concerned, but by 1928 the Chancellor, the cabinet and two members of the Reichstag's budgetary committee were also informed so that awkward questions in parliament might be avoided.[6]

In December 1927 Defence Minister Gessler resigned and was replaced by General Groener, who had played such an important part in shaping the destinies of the officer corps after the November revolution.[7] A general himself, he was in a stronger position than Gessler *vis-à-vis* his military colleagues. He had no time for counter-revolutionary tendencies among his soldiers. On the other hand Groener was not a democratic general. He was willing to work with the Social Democrats, for example, because he no longer feared 'Marxism', having witnessed its impotence during the revolution. Communism now seemed to him to be the real enemy. Yet he would not tolerate socialist or pacifist criticism of the army, nor would he permit parliamentary pressure to restrict its activities. Collaboration with parliament was a one-way affair.[8]

Fundamentally the army had changed very little since 1919. The officer corps was overwhelmingly anti-Republican. Recruitment remained restricted very largely to men of nationalist or apolitical backgrounds, most of them from rural areas. At a local level – especially in regions controlled by Social Democrats – relations with the civilian authorities remained unhappy.

Nor can it be claimed that other German institutions, such as the civil service and the judiciary, developed anything approaching a Republican *esprit de corps* in these years of stability. Collaboration with the existing authorities was necessary because there was no alternative, but enthusiasm was lacking. In Germany's universities many of the students and their professors regarded the Weimar system with contempt. As the twenties wore on, so projects for the reform of the State to give it a more authoritarian form of government began to be heard. There was a general call for 'strong leadership', and this affected many political groups. By 1928 the Republic's four years of peace had not produced the impression of stability. One right-wing intellectual journal *Tat* summed up a widely-held attitude when it wrote: 'These times long for authority, they are tired of liberal ideals.'⁹

Much criticism was directed at the parliamentary system itself, and there can be no doubt that it suffered from serious defects. Most of these were due not so much to its liberal character, as to the weakness of Germany's political parties.

As we have seen, these inherited a sectional or class character from the former German Empire, and attempts to widen their appeal had never been successful. The so-called Weimar Coalition of Centre, Democrats and Social Democrats had always been subject to tensions over class interest and religion. Hence the appeal of any single Republican party was necessarily limited, and there was no chance of it being entrusted with full responsibility for the nation's government.

Even the Social Democratic Party, the most whole-hearted defender of the Republican system, was torn between a desire to protect the interests of wage-earners and its responsibility for the safety of German democracy. When Paul Löbe, the Socialist Reichstag President (speaker), wrote in May 1927 that the real issue was not 'Republic versus monarchy' but 'capitalism versus socialism', he was stressing the divisions between Social Democracy and the bourgeois liberal parties.[10] Yet many of his colleagues, especially those with ministerial experience like the Prussian Premier, Otto Braun, believed that Social Democrats should do all they could to share administrative power so that the Republic could be governed by those who were emotionally attached to it.

There is nothing unusual, or particularly disgraceful, about the expression of material interests through political parties. But such sectional objectives cannot become the overriding concern of political leadership if government is to work effectively. As it was, the compromises and bargaining between coalition groups necessary before a government could hope to obtain parliamentary support made consistent policies on major issues difficult to achieve unless ministers treated parliament as of secondary importance. Instead of the Republican parties forming a united front when faced with critical problems, they often simply agreed to differ, leaving responsibility to be shouldered by their ministerial colleagues.

In the middle years of Republican development such an arrangement put Reich Chancellors in a very weak position *vis-à-vis* the coalition parties, since they had to agree to a series of concessions in order to hold their governments together at all. The support given to ministries by parliament was often tepid in the extreme. Although it was envisaged in the constitution that cabinets should command the confidence of a Reichstag majority, only two out of five were given a formal vote of confidence between 1924 and 1928. Two of the others received what was described as a 'declaration of acceptance' and the third had to make do with a statement that the Reichstag 'took note' of its existence.[11]

Under these circumstances it was not surprising that the gulf between the Reichstag and ministerial leaders grew wider, that the influence of the President became more important, and that the successes of government were attributed not so much to political parties, as to civil servants and to 'expert' ministers.

The weaknesses in the party system here described did not necessarily mean that Germany's parliamentary system was doomed to failure. Had the country been vouchsafed a longer period of economic and international stability, it is possible that more effective forms of parliamentary co-operation might have been found. But this is a matter for speculation. What is clear is that, even during an apparently calm interlude, the relationship between Reichstag parties, ministers and President was not developing in a manner designed to strengthen those forces in the State which were loyal to the Republic. The stature of parliamentary institutions was being diminished in the public mind.

In the summer of 1928 such a forecast of doom for the parliamentary system would have seemed pessimistic. With the appearance of a Social Democratic Chancellor, Hermann Müller, Republican fortunes seemed to be on an upward curve. But the elections of that year had actually brought no real improvement in the parliamentary situation. The new Chancellor lacked the qualities to inspire his followers or to make a great public impact as a national leader. He had to take office without firm pledges of support from a parliamentary majority, even though his ministry included men from all the major Republican parties. He was soon in the humiliating position of being forced to vote against the policy of his own cabinet by order of his party's Reichstag delegation. This occurred because the Government felt unable to honour a Socialist election pledge that the size of the military budget would be cut.

There were other dark spots on the horizon. The elections had been a severe blow to the German Nationalists, who were once again forced into opposition. There had always been conflicts between those in the Nationalist Party who wanted to concentrate on attacking the Republic, and those who were more interested in influencing the conduct of the government – particularly in economic affairs. After failure at the elections, the intransigent elements gained the upper hand. They were personified in the figure of Alfred Hugenberg, an industrialist turned newspaper proprietor. His views on the political course to be followed by the DNVP had already been summed up the previous year in a letter to von Westarp, when he remarked that no Nationalist could adapt himself to the Republican system. One who did, he claimed, 'becomes a genuine parliamentarian, and that is the same as a German Democrat . . . a cripple in his heart'.[12] Hugenberg refused to be a 'cripple'. He wanted a united, disciplined party, absolutely loyal to its leader. Not surprisingly, he felt himself called to exercise this leadership, and he had the means to obtain it.

In the autumn of 1928 the Nationalist Party was demoralised and short of funds. Hugenberg offered it financial aid and the propaganda machine which lay to hand in his own newspaper empire. The party felt it had little choice and, in any case, many welcomed a swing to the right. The former leader, Count von Westarp, had to yield, and Hugenberg took over. The policy of the DNVP now became one of strident and unrestrained opposition to the Republic.

At the end of the year a change also took place in the leadership of the Centre Party. Marx, a former candidate for the Presidency who had headed more than one Reich coalition, retired. A Roman Catholic priest, prelate Kaas, was elected leader by a narrow majority. Kaas, who had close links with the Vatican, was less interested in political collaboration with Republican parties than in the defence of his religion. On the whole he found conservative social groups, especially those associated with the maintenance of law and order, preferable to atheist Social Democrats or free-thinking liberals. The Centre Party's parliamentary delegation came under the direction of a young ex-officer, Heinrich Brüning. He represented a generation to which the manœuvrings in the Reichstag seemed outmoded and unattractive. These developments, within a party which had always been one of Weimar's most constant political supports, were to have important consequences.

The year 1928 seemed to bring with it the prospects of further progress on the reparations question.

In February 1929 a committee of experts – this time including Germans – met to discusss a final plan for reparations. It was headed by Owen Young, formerly Vice-Chairman of the Dawes Committee. After some heated negotiations, a Plan was produced whereby Germany would pay reparations until 1988. The payments would rise from 1·7 thousand million marks in 1930, to 2·4 thousand million in 1966. After that they would diminish. In return, Germany was to be financially independent. Controls over her railways and banking system were dropped. She was no longer to enjoy the protection of an Allied agent in the field of transfer. On the other hand, some provision was made for the postponement of one-third of any given annuity in case of emergency, and another third could always be paid in kind.

As with the Dawes Plan, the Young scheme – put into its final form at the end of August 1929[13] – presupposed a period of general economic growth and stability. By the summer of 1929 signs were already apparent that such optimistic forecasts were unwarranted. Unemployment remained ominously high, and investment was falling. The scheme aroused furious opposition from the German Nationalists. They felt that it set the seal on Germany's defeat. It seemed to mortgage the future for generations, and by establishing a final settlement, it would undermine the German will to destroy the Versailles Treaty. Even the promise given to Stresemann by the French at the end of August 1929 that the Rhineland would be evacuated in 1930 – five years ahead of schedule – did nothing to dampen their fury. It was not the terms but the whole concept of a settlement which they rejected.

Alfred Hugenberg eagerly took the lead in opposing the Young Plan. He coupled his assault on it with a campaign against the 'war guilt lie' and the whole Republican system. In July 1929 a committee was established to organise a right-wing front against the Plan. In it were represented Hugenberg's Nationalist Party, the Stahlhelm, the Pan-German league and Hitler's Nazi Party. The latter group was an unusual ally to be recruited into what was otherwise a socially conservative and backward-looking movement. But Hugenberg found Hitler's unrestrained assaults on the Weimar system attractive, and he thought that his dynamic oratory, together with the youth and enthusiasm present in the Nazi Party, would materially assist the Nationalist cause. Hugenberg, like others of his background and political persuasion, saw Hitler as a 'drummer' who would whip up popular support for a campaign controlled by his social superiors. It was a grievous miscalculation.

Hitler benefited greatly from the alliance; Hugenberg not at all. By association with the German Nationalists and their friends, the Nazis gained an aura of respectability they had lacked before. Even more important was the publicity given them by the Hugenberg press, which was far more widely read than the miserably unsuccessful Nazi papers. Hitler also came into contact with men of wealth and influence who could be of great material help to his party.

Hugenberg, on the other hand, simply increased the tensions within his own following which had already been growing as the result of his new tactics within the DNVP. The *Führerprinzip** demanded complete obedience to the leader's authority. Many local organisations, as well as some Reichstag members, were loath to submit themselves in this way and the alliance with Hitler aroused even more discontent among moderate sections of the Nationalist Party.

The campaign against the Young Plan culminated in December 1929 with a plebiscite which registered 5·8 million

* Literally 'leadership principle'.

votes in favour of Hugenberg's anti-Young proposals. This was well short of the 21 millions needed for success, but the campaign had ensured that the Young Plan was received in Germany, not as a triumph of Republican diplomacy, but as at best an expedient, at worst a national humiliation.[14]

Indeed, there were good reasons for nervousness about Germany's economic future if the Plan was implemented. The Plan had been accepted in principle at a conference in The Hague in August 1929, but it was not finally signed by President Hindenburg until the following spring. During the intervening months there had been a catastrophic change in the country's economic prospects. The optimistic assumptions which underlay the terms of the Plan were no longer compatible with reality. Hopes that somehow the boom of the previous two years might return were completely shattered by the Wall Street stock market crash in October 1929. Its impact on the Germans was bound to be disastrous. Loss of confidence engendered by the slump in America meant that surplus funds were no longer available for investment in Germany.

Even before the slump in America the German stock market had been declining. Unemployment had risen to an average of nearly two million in 1929. The Government was divided over measures to raise revenue.

On the issue of unemployment the German People's Party and the Social Democrats were naturally inclined to opposite points of view. Employers blamed the recession on high wages and high taxes; the trade unions argued that real wages were still low and that industrial profits should be ploughed back into industry. The unemployment insurance scheme set up in 1927 had placed a heavy tax burden on the State. It had not been assumed that unemployment would rise, and contributions were thus not high enough to meet the benefits which had to be paid out. The employers and their allies – especially the German

People's Party – thought that the burden ought to fall on those receiving benefits, while the trade unions fought for larger contributions from industry.

The People's Party itself had moved strongly to the right in 1929, a tendency that had been aided by Stresemann's failing health. Worn down by a kidney disease, he died on 3 October 1929. This was a severe blow for the Republic, but it is by no means clear that Stresemann could have kept his party from breaking with the Social Democrats even had he lived.[15] For their part, the Social Democrats showed little realisation of the nature of the crisis which faced them. They put loyalty to their class before loyalty to the Republican coalition.

The wrangling within the cabinet added strength to those in German public life who were demanding reform of the entire Weimar system. The cry for strong leadership grew more insistent. It found receptive ears in the Bendlerstrasse, where Defence Minister Groener and his chief political adviser, General von Schleicher, had decided that Müller's government would have to go. They wanted a cabinet which could be relied upon to protect the Reichswehr's interests in a time of crisis. They wanted to see the moderate element in the German Nationalist Party brought back into the Government at the expense of the Social Democrats. Above all, they envisaged a government which would not have to rely on the constantly shifting forces in the Reichstag. Instead, the emergency powers of the President would be invoked to impose ministerial authority on the nation.[16]

The final conflict came over financial policy. The Social Democrats and the People's Party were at loggerheads. The former were determined that the burden of sacrifice in a critical situation should not fall on the unemployed, whose dole payments were an obvious target for administrative economy. Ministers of both parties would have been ready for a compromise; their Reichstag colleagues preferred to make a break. An attempt by Chancellor Müller to enlist

presidential aid was rejected by Hindenburg.[17] On 27
March 1930 Müller resigned. No other government ruled
Germany on the basis of a parliamentary majority until
Hitler took power with the intention of destroying German
democracy.

Müller's fall has sometimes been seen as the termination
of democratic government in Germany, and 27 March 1930
as the date on which the Republic really expired.[18] This is
an unduly fatalistic view. There was nothing unusual in the
appearance of a minority government, and the use of
presidential decrees during an emergency had respectable
precedents.[19] There were certainly strong tendencies among
the non-socialist parties in favour of structural reforms in
Germany which would strengthen the executive against
parliament, and it was natural that at a time of crisis there
should be a widespread yearning for stability. But this was
far from being a rejection of constitutional government.
None of those who played a part in engineering the fall of
Müller's cabinet could have had any idea that their action
would help to bring about the rise of Adolf Hitler.

In the spring of 1930 the Nazis did not seem a very
serious danger, even though their party had sprung into
prominence during the campaign against the Young Plan.
They only held twelve seats in the Reichstag. As a bogey
they could not be used to frighten politicians. The Communist Party, on the other hand, looked more formidable,
especially to the Social Democrats, who were its main rivals
for working-class support. Since 1928 the Communists, now
largely controlled from Moscow, had been following a line
of violent hostility towards the Social Democrats, dubbing
them 'social fascists'. Unemployment naturally seemed to
work in favour of the Communists. Many in the SPD felt
that unless their party stopped seeing itself as a pillar of the
Government, and began to act as a representative of the
working class, it would lose its mass support. The threat
from the right was not very frightening. Hugenberg's

leadership was wrecking the German Nationalist Party; Hitler was still regarded with contempt.

On the right General von Schleicher believed that his intrigues would strengthen conservative forces in Germany while isolating the Hugenberg wing of the German Nationalist Party. The non-socialist parties in the coalition had become less and less happy about collaboration with 'Marxists', and they had no reason to feel that union to save democracy was imperative. The Weimar 'system' was judged to have failed. It was thought that a strong government based on presidential power would be needed to steer Germany through the crisis. This did not necessarily imply the end of constitutional government. Brüning, the new Chancellor, himself had no thought of establishing a dictatorship, even though he would clearly face difficulties in the Reichstag if Müller's party insisted on opposing him. He had formerly been willing to collaborate with the Social Democrats. Now he had to form a cabinet without them. His government included all the other parties of the former coalition, and representatives of some splinter parties on the right. Nevertheless, without the SPD the Government possessed no parliamentary majority.

Brüning made it clear that he would press through a programme of financial retrenchment by the use of presidential decrees if necessary. Opposition in the Reichstag would be answered by a dissolution. The Social Democrats, who did not wish to face elections at that moment, would have been willing to make a compromise agreement with Brüning, but this would have endangered his new coalition. In any case, the real forces behind the new Chancellor – the President and the army – would not have tolerated such a shift to the left.

Brüning pressed on with his programme, suffered defeat in the Reichstag as the result of Social Democratic opposition, and dissolved parliament. Germany faced a general election two years earlier than would normally have been the case. It was an election which brought small comfort to Brüning – his government parties could barely hold their own. But it was a triumph for another young German leader. Adolf Hitler's Nazis returned 107 members to the Reichstag. National Socialism was now a political force which could not be ignored.

[1] Dorpalen, *Hindenburg*, p. 143.
[2] The official figure was 1284 million RM. See Luke, *Stabilisierung*, p. 92.
[3] Born, *Bankenkrise*, pp. 29–30.
[4] Ibid. p. 18.
[5] Carsten, *Reichswehr*, p. 267.
[6] Ibid. pp. 273–5.
[7] Ibid. pp. 24 ff.
[8] Ibid. pp. 290–6.
[9] Curt Hölzel, *Tat*, xx, 1928, quoted in Dorpalen, *Hindenburg*, p. 164.
[10] Dorpalen, *Hindenburg*, p. 119.
[11] Stürmer, 'Probleme der parlamentarischen Mehrheitsbildung in der Stabilisierungsphase der Weimarer Republik', p. 80.
[12] Quoted by Chanady in 'The Disintegration of the German National People's Party, 1924–1930', p. 81. The entire article, pp. 65–91, is illuminating on the tragic development of the German Nationalist Party at the end of the Republican era. See also Hiller von Gaertringen, 'Die Deutschnationale Volkspartei', in *Das Ende der Parteien* (eds. Matthias–Morsey) pp. 543–56.
[13] With some modifications owing to British opposition, Germany had to guarantee payment of a rather large part of the annuities unconditionally, and had to agree to pay part of the Allies occupation costs. These did not, in any case, last very long.
[14] See Bullock, *Hitler*, pp. 147–9; Bracher, *Auflösung*, pp. 290–1, 316–22.
[15] For Stresemann's difficulties with his party in 1929, see Turner, *Stresemann*, pp. 250–1, 267.
[16] For accounts of the crisis in the early months of 1930 see Bracher, *Auflösung*, pp. 287–389, Conze–Raupach, *Staats- und Wirtschaftskrise*, pp. 176 ff.; Dorpalen, *Hindenburg*, pp. 163–78; Wheeler-Bennett, *Hindenburg*, pp. 336–49. The latter account was based on personal acquaintance with and information from nany of the leading participants in the crisis. Although in some minor particulars it has been superseded by time, its main interpretations have been fully borne out by more recent research.

[17] Dorpalen, *Hindenburg*, pp. 175–6.

[18] Heiber, *Republik von Weimar*, p. 218. See also Rosenberg, *German Republic*, pp. 300 ff., in which the Brüning era is described as the beginning of the triumph of counter-revolution.

[19] In November–December 1923, for example.

10 The End of the Republic

WHAT of Hitler in the years of stability? He had experienced imprisonment and a return to political obscurity. But he had not been deflected from his purpose. His years in the wilderness had been well spent, building up the party machine which was to carry him to power.

During his trial for high treason at Munich in April 1924 he was allowed by nationally-minded Bavarian judges to launch a fierce attack on the whole Republican system. He did not attempt to excuse his role in the Munich Putsch. On the contrary, he gloried in it. His more respectable collaborators in the conflict with Berlin – von Kahr, von Lossow and von Seisser – were called as witnesses for the prosecution, and had to pretend that they were not responsible for what had happened. By contrast Hitler appeared as a fearless, honest leader willing to take the consequences for his actions:

'I alone bear the responsibility', he boasted, 'but I am not a criminal because of that. If today I stand here as a revolutionary, it is as a revolutionary against the revolution. There is no such thing as High Treason against the traitors of 1918.'[1] This brave stand made his former colleagues in the conspiracy look wretched indeed, and it was far more impressive than the behaviour of the leaders of the Kapp Putsch in 1920.

Hitler was sentenced to five years imprisonment – the minimum possible for the charge on which he had been arraigned. Even then it was made clear that he would be pardoned well before the end of his sentence. He was incarcerated at Landsberg, a small town west of Munich.

His treatment was generous in the extreme; very different from the harsh conditions imposed on those Socialists and Communists who had been tried after the crushing of the Munich Soviet five years earlier.

It was in prison that Hitler dictated *Mein Kampf.* This book – part autobiography and part political treatise – was one of Hitler's main sources of personal income in the lean years which followed the Putsch. After his rise to political prominence in 1930 it became a best-seller. Max Amann, Hitler's business manager, was the publisher of the book, and credit with him served as Hitler's only bank account. Amann was to be well rewarded. In the Third Reich his Nazi publishing house came to control a lion's share of the German press.[2]

Mein Kampf was a long, rambling and badly written book which demonstrated that Hitler's gifts as an orator could not easily be turned to literary purposes. It contained many errors of punctuation, style and grammar which were only gradually eliminated in later editions. Changes in substance, however, were less noticeable and this bore witness to the relative consistency of Hitler's thought. In only one particular did he make any serious modification. A reference to 'Germanic Democracy' in the organisation of the Nazi Party was deleted, and replaced with a passage stressing the need for unconditional obedience to the Leader. This too was perfectly in keeping with Hitler's political behaviour from the very beginning of his career.[3]

Generally speaking the book mirrored Hitler's character and fundamental attitudes faithfully enough. His belief in the right of the strong to dominate the weak, his violent racialism, his fascination with the techniques of mass manipulation and his contempt for the masses themselves, all found lengthy – if unconvincing – expression.

He was released from prison in time for Christmas 1924. The Nazi Party was in a bad state after his absence, partly because he had deliberately refrained from appointing an effective deputy. Rivalries had appeared between different personalities and there were ideological conflicts within the Nazi movement. One of the most able and energetic Bavarian leaders, Gregor Strasser, had been conducting a successful campaign to build up the party's strength in north Germany. Working-class elements were more strongly represented in the North German Nazi movement than in Bavaria. North Germans were suspicious of the Roman Catholic South and resented the dictatorial attitude of the party headquarters in Munich. They disliked some of the more disreputable figures who seemed to be influential there, such as Hermann Esser and Julius Streicher.

By the beginning of 1926 these frictions had been compounded by arguments over policy. Some of the North German Nazis wanted more open attacks on capitalism and rejected parliamentary activity. They pressed for participation in the campaign being organised by Communists and Social Democrats to dispossess the former German royal houses. Hitler would have none of this. Although originally opposed to parliamentary tactics, he had decided that the party must keep to the paths of legality if it was to survive. He had no interest in social revolution for its own sake, and realised that such radical programmes would simply frighten the propertied classes. There followed a confrontation in which Hitler was victorious in every respect.

In February 1926 Strasser and his friends capitulated, being consoled with some changes in the personnel at party headquarters. One of Strasser's young sympathisers, an ambitious orator called Josef Goebbels, was completely won over to Hitler. He was later sent to Berlin to eliminate the influence of Strasserites there.

Hitler's victory ensured that the Nazi movement remained true to its Bavarian origins in both its ideology and its organisation. At a party congress in May 1926 its programme was declared immutable. This helped to muffle theoretical discussions which might deflect the party from its true purpose, the seizure of power.[4]

The next few years were difficult ones. Political stability and economic recovery were no help to Hitler's party, and in the Reichstag elections of 1928 it only won twelve seats. It was still most strongly supported in Bavaria – especially in the Protestant Franconian province, where the Nazis received over 8 per cent of the poll. But this was a very weak performance compared with that of the ruling Bavarian People's Party, and the Bavarian Social Democrats fared much better than the Nazis. The party seemed on its way to permanent obscurity.

Nevertheless, it still possessed some advantages. It was young – its age structure compared very favourably in this respect with all parties except the Communists. It was apparently classless. It had never been compromised by exercising power in the Republic, nor was it associated with monarchism. The Nazis could attack 'reaction' in their speeches with as much verve as when they castigated the Jews or the Marxists. Unlike the Communists they did not threaten property, nor were they controlled by a foreign power. On the contrary, a strident nationalism was a fundamental element in their appeal.

After 1928 this appeal began to find a more sympathetic hearing throughout Germany. The self-evident weaknesses in the parliamentary system damaged the authority of the Republican State. The defeat of the German National People's Party, and the subsequent divisions within it, made Hitler's movement seem at once both respectable and more effective. Above all, the growth in unemployment and economic uncertainty led to a radicalisation of public attitudes towards politics. Hitler was the most obvious beneficiary of Germany's new troubles.

As we have seen, his first great political opportunity came with the campaign against the Young Plan, when his alliance with Hugenberg's group enabled him to obtain

F

publicity in the Nationalist press and to make contact with men of wealth and social position. The result of such contacts, and of a growth in party membership, was reflected in the new affluence of Hitler's party in Munich, where the Nazis moved into more imposing premises – the 'Brown House'. Money was also available for propaganda and the expansion of the SA.

By the autumn of 1930 the Nazis were ready for greater triumphs. Their membership was rising; their finances in a healthier state than ever before. They had begun to make a concerted attempt to woo the German farmer, whose economic security was apparently being undermined by the slump. Walther Darré, a racialist with a romantic vision of the German peasantry as the backbone of the Nordic German *Volk*, drew up a Nazi agrarian programme which was published in March 1930. The Nazis told the farmers what they wanted to hear; that they represented a way of life which should be preserved, no matter what the economic situation. Rural life was morally superior to urban life and should be protected from the vicissitudes of a market economy.

Armed with this message of hope to the farming community, benefiting from the newly radical atmosphere created by the slump and harping on national resentments which became stronger as Germany's domestic situation grew more hopeless, the Nazis won a resounding triumph at the polls. With over 18 per cent of the vote and 107 seats in the Reichstag they were the second largest party in Germany. The Social Democrats remained in first place, but on their left the Communists had also made big gains. The Centre Party had held its position, but all the other Republican groups had fared very badly. Hugenberg's DNVP had lost over two million votes – almost half its previous total – and its representation in parliament fell from 73 to 41. His Nationalists were now in a position of inferiority *vis-à-vis* Hitler's Nazis in the anti-Republican right.

The election showed that the Nazis had broken out of their older regional boundaries and had gained support throughout the country. In particular, it was noticeable that in those places where there had been most votes cast in the anti-Young referendum the Nazis produced the best election results some nine months later. In the eastern and northern areas of Germany as well as in Franconia they polled heavily. Schleswig-Holstein, a region of small farmers whose security was threatened by indebtedness and foreign competition, gave them their best result, with 27 per cent of the total vote.[5] The association with Hugenberg's anti-Young campaign and the appeal to the farmers had brought rich rewards. The Nazis also benefited from increased participation in elections provoked by the atmosphere of crisis. Together with an increase in the size of the electorate, this meant that four million more votes were cast in 1930 than in 1928. A high percentage of these went to the Nazis.

Chancellor Brüning faced a difficult situation after the September elections. His hopes of a Centre-Right victory were dashed, and it was clear that the new Reichstag would be even more difficult to work with than the old one. On the other hand, the two main opposition parties in the previous parliament – the Social Democrats and the German Nationalists – had fared much worse at the polls than Brüning's own coalition group. Arrangements with them seemed a real possibility.

This hope was justified in the case of the Social Democrats. The dramatic Nazi gains in the elections had come to them as a shocking surprise. They reacted with a sharpness which verged on panic. Whereas before the election they had seen German politics as an economic struggle between rich and poor, they now realised that the whole structure of their parliamentary Republic was in jeopardy. One result of this anxiety was a revival of enthusiasm for the Reichsbanner, which had tended to lose its militancy after the 1928 elections. Prominent Social Democrats now announced their adherence to it, and the Reichsbanner as a whole prepared to wage a much more vigorous battle against Hitler's SA.[6] Some leaders of the SPD wanted to make common cause with Brüning in the Government. Support for such a move came from industrial and banking circles, where it was feared that the extremist gains in the elections would damage Germany's international standing. But no coalition resulted.

Brüning could not move to the left without encountering the opposition of the President and the Reichswehr. Coalition with the Social Democrats would also have made collaboration with the People's Party and the moderate Nationalist groups very difficult. In any case, Brüning was able to win the tacit support of the Social Democrats without taking them into his government. Their leaders agreed not to overthrow him in the Reichstag, and this meant that he could continue to rule by emergency decree without parliament intervening against him.[7]

Attempts to win support for the Government from Hugenberg's Nationalists and the ex-soldiers' association, the Stahlhelm, proved much more disappointing. Hugenberg maintained an unyielding attitude. He demanded that, as a price for his collaboration, the Prussian government should be reconstructed to eliminate the Social Democrats. This was an unrealistic condition, since the Nationalist group in the Reichstag could in no way replace the voting power of the Social Democrats. The Stahlhelm seemed at first more amenable to Brüning's overtures, but their hatred of the Republican system got the better of them and they stayed aloof.[8]

Hindenburg regretted the failure of these right-wing groups to support Brüning, but he did not distance himself from them as a result. Their influence continued to be felt in the presidential palace, and in the ranks of the army. Although Hindenburg was loyal to Brüning throughout 1931, he and his military advisers disliked a situation in which they had to rely on the Social Democrats for the stability of their régime. As the year wore on and conditions grew more critical, an arrangement which would include the Nazis in a genuinely nationalist government seemed more and more attractive.

The root cause of the severe political stresses which troubled Germany was economic. 1929 had seen the beginning of the Great Depression. It continued to gather momentum in the years which followed. Share prices fell steadily and bank reserves dwindled. Germany, dependent as she was on foreign credits for her economic health, was especially vulnerable to a crisis of confidence which affected the whole world. Unemployment, already at crisis level in 1929, rose catastrophically as the slump grew worse. By February 1931 there were nearly five million registered unemployed and a year later the figure was well over six millions. The crisis meant ruin for many small businessmen and farmers, and even threatened the security of larger concerns.

Brüning showed great courage in tackling these problems, but he was not able to offer the German people very much positive encouragement. His policies always seemed to involve sacrifice rather than hope. They also included a number of glaring anomalies made necessary by his attachment to the conservative forces around the President. Despite large cuts in government spending the military budget remained relatively high. The Reichswehr was too powerful to be treated like other departments of state.

Others to receive preferential treatment were large landowners in Eastern Germany. These were among the least efficient farmers in the country, and many of their estates were heavily mortgaged. The President, himself an East Prussian landowner, had always shown a lively interest in their welfare. The eastern provinces were Germany's wheat-growing areas, and in order to protect their home market heavy duties were placed on imported grain. While unemployment benefit was being cut, wages and salaries reduced and industrial prices forced down, the cost of bread and cereals was maintained at an artificially high level. Grain cost 250 per cent more in Germany than it could be purchased on the world market. So the cost of living – especially for the poor – fell less sharply than the level of incomes. In addition, a financial burden was placed on German industry to provide cheap credit for the East Elbean farmers. This meant that one of the least efficient parts of the German economy was being propped up by an industrial sector which was itself desperately short of capital. Meanwhile, other sections of German agriculture – the smaller proprietors with mixed and dairy farms – were left relatively unprotected and had to pay an inflated price for their grain. The incomes from their farms fell spectacularly, and in desperation many of them turned to the Nazis for salvation.[9] It was a situation which prompted one distinguished economist to exclaim: 'I do not understand this policy. Do we want a social revolution?'[10]

Brüning certainly did not want a social revolution. His harsh policies were designed to shield Germany from worse catastrophe. The preferences given to the Eastern landowners and the military were unfortunate, especially since both groups were strongly opposed to the Republic which supported them. Nevertheless, it is difficult to believe that savings on these items alone could have righted the German economy.

The Depression posed agonising problems for all governments which had to grapple with it, and few of them survived the test.* Brüning, who had considerable experience of financial and economic matters, adopted methods of dealing with the crisis similar to those used in other countries. His policy was one of stringent economy and

---

* To take the most obvious examples, President Hoover was defeated in the American election in 1932 and Ramsay MacDonald's Labour government collapsed in August 1931.

deflation. Owing to the fall in the national income caused by the slump, tax receipts were falling. Hence very severe measures had to be taken to reduce spending and raise taxes. In July 1930 new taxes were imposed and a special levy placed on people in public employment. By the end of the year there was still a deficit of 1200 million Reichsmarks. Brüning then started imposing price cuts on government contractors, and during 1931 public employees had their pay reduced by a total of 23 per cent. In January and December 1931 there were compulsory price cuts for cartelised industrial products. With the second of these reductions wages were pegged back to the level of January 1927. A National Price Commissioner was established to ensure that these measures bore fruit.

In the years which followed the Great Depression it became fashionable to attack such deflationary policies as counter-productive. There were successful government spending programmes in Hitler's Germany and Roosevelt's America. The economic theories of J. M. Keynes seemed to prove that the way to defeat unemployment and recession was to increase the purchasing power, even if this involved reducing the value of the currency and risking inflation.

Brüning was far too orthodox an economist to run such risks. It is as well to remember that Keynes's *The General Theory of Employment, Interest and Money* did not appear until 1936. Most informed opinion in 1930 would have supported Brüning's deflationary tactics. Trade union leaders as well as businessmen were agreed that there had to be cuts – they simply argued that the burden should fall on capitalists rather than the unemployed. It was believed that reductions in wages could produce proportionately heavier falls in prices, thus causing consumption to rise.[11] Inflation was seen as Germany's worst enemy; the memories of 1923 were still very much alive.

Brüning's policies may well have exaggerated the crisis and caused unemployment to rise more than was necessary.

But a more ambitious course might have led to a complete collapse of the mark. There is no evidence that, even with a perfectly free hand, Brüning could have helped Germany to survive the depression by pursuing – in isolation from the rest of the world – a policy of reflation.

In any case, his hands were not free. Germany was in a special position economically because of her reparations debts. The Young Plan, created in an atmosphere of economic optimism, had put very specific restrictions on Germany's credit system. Under the agreement implementing the Plan Germany had pledged herself to maintain the value of the mark. Whenever discreet hints were dropped in Washington and Paris that it might be necessary to revoke this pledge they were met with forthright and unyielding resistance.[12]

Brüning was determined to end reparations, both because of their damage to the German economy and because he thought that success in foreign policy would win his government the popular support it badly needed. If the Allies were to be made to see that Germany could no longer continue meeting its obligations under the Young Plan, he would have to demonstrate that she was pursuing a policy of rigorous economy. He could not afford to indulge in work-creation schemes or other palliatives for unemployment lest his reparations creditors should claim they were not being given first priority. It was the old policy of 'fulfilment' carried to its most logical conclusion.

For Germany to reach a satisfactory settlement of her reparations difficulties there would have to be a willingness to make concessions among her former enemies. By the summer of 1929 Stresemann had managed to win considerable prestige in the West, and in Aristide Briand he had found a sympathetic French counterpart. But after Stresemann's death the situation deteriorated. His successor, Curtius, was a less skilful diplomatist and felt the need for quick results to please opinion at home. As German politics took a turn towards the right, so the public posture of Germany's leaders had to grow more nationalistic.

The Chancellor's own major objectives lay in the fields of reparations and armaments. Brüning hoped to win relief from the former and equality over the latter. Friction with the French did not help his cause, nor did the aggressive tone of German domestic politics. One historian has described Brüning's policy as 'an attempt to appear nationalist at home and conciliatory abroad'.[13] Unfortunately for the Chancellor, it was impossible to hide the resurgence of German nationalism from the eyes of the world, nor could his meagre successes in the field of foreign affairs appease domestic critics.

In fact, the year 1931 saw the end of reparations. The British government, worried by Britain's deteriorating trade figures, wanted to write off reparations and inter-Allied war debts. The gravity of the situation in Germany and Austria – where the leading private bank collapsed in May – caused the Americans to revise their policy. On 20 June President Hoover suddenly announced a moratorium on inter-Allied debts on condition that reparations payments were also suspended. This really ended German payments to the Allies. It did not, however, solve the country's immediate financial problems. The bankruptcy of a textile combine caused one of Germany's largest banks to close its doors. The Government once again had to step in with emergency measures, including exchange control.

Reparations were indeed dead, but the manner of their passing brought no kudos to Brüning. The moratorium was supposed to be temporary and came as a gift from America. It was not a diplomatic triumph for Berlin. The economic crisis remained and was growing worse. German diplomacy – affected as it was by the need to succour national pride – did not contribute to an atmosphere of international collaboration and confidence, without which the world's economic problems could not be overcome. The Germans did nothing, for example, to respond to French suggestions that 'a political moratorium' should accompany that on reparations. This would have involved the dropping of Germany's revisionist posture and reductions in her arms budget. But such measures would never have been tolerated, either by the Government parties or by the Reichswehr.

Nevertheless, by the spring of 1932 Brüning's two major objectives seemed near to achievement. Reparations were suspended and there was every chance that they would never reappear. Negotiations at Geneva on the question of disarmament had revealed widespread willingness among the powers to give Germany the equal status she had been demanding for so long. Brüning afterwards claimed that in Spring 1932 he had almost attained his goal.[14] It was a goal he never reached. At the end of May he was dismissed. His successors, von Papen and von Schleicher, reaped the fruits of his policies. At the Lausanne Conference in July 1932 Germany's creditors agreed to renounce almost 90 per cent of their former claims if their own war debts received similarly magnanimous treatment. In fact Germany never paid any more reparations at all. The following December Germany's equal status in the field of armaments was recognised by most of her former enemies.

Lausanne

It has been argued that if these concessions had been granted to Brüning before his fall he could have overcome Germany's political crisis. There is very little reason to believe this. His dismissal was not the result of diplomatic failures. Nor did subsequent successes over reparations and disarmament bring much comfort to the luckless Chancellors who followed him.

The immediate causes of Brüning's fall were entirely political. Not having received his mandate as Chancellor from the Reichstag and still less from the electorate, he was dependent on the good-will of his real supporters – President Hindenburg and the army. By the beginning of 1932 this was a very unsure foundation upon which to base a government. General von Schleicher was very disappointed that Brüning had not overcome the opposition of the Nationalists and had to rely on Social Democratic forbearance in the Reichstag. He wanted to see the Social Democrats ejected from their position of power in Prussia. So he began to feel that some sort of accommodation with the Nazis might be desirable. Hitler was only too willing to encourage this attitude, though he was careful never to compromise his own independence.

Brüning himself wanted no truck with Hitler. But his position was being undermined. Hindenburg – his mind burdened by the constant complaints of his Nationalist acquaintances – was beginning to lose confidence in the Chancellor. In March 1932 the President had to face re-election. Efforts by Brüning to persuade the Nationalist opposition to allow the old field-marshal to be returned unopposed failed.

March 1932 Presidential election

The presidential election campaign revealed an extraordinary reversal of political roles since the previous contest in 1925. Then it had been the parties of the right which had supported Hindenburg. The Weimar Coalition parties – Democrats, Centre and Social Democrats – had provided his most serious opposition. Only the very extreme racialists gave their votes to General Ludendorff. By 1932 the political landscape had been transformed. The Republican parties, together with the more cautious conservative groups represented in Brüning's government, campaigned for Hindenburg. The mass of his votes would come from the Social Democrats and the Roman Catholic Centre Party. His old supporters among the German Nationalists and the Stahlhelm had turned their backs on him. They ran their own candidate, the radically anti-Republican Duesterberg, who was second-in-command of the Stahlhelm. It was clear that Duesterberg was not going to be a powerful challenge to Hindenburg, and that most votes on the right would go to

Hitler. The other serious candidate was Thälmann for the Communist Party.

Hitler himself had hesitated before entering the battle. The Nazi Party was by no means invincible. It was not even the largest in the Reichstag. Hindenburg would be very difficult to beat. Nevertheless, the party had been making impressive progress. Its membership was growing fast and the SA was mushrooming also. By the end of 1931 there were over 300,000 brown-shirted SA men available for demonstrations, marches and street fights with opponents. A growth in mass support meant an increase in funds. It also attracted wealthy donors. In the early months of 1932 Hitler was successful in persuading a number of industrialists and financiers that his assaults on democracy were easily compatible with capitalism. Although Hitler was never the tool of any vested interest, his success in gaining funds from business circles was important at this stage in the party's development.[15]*

Once the election campaign got under way the Nazis' propaganda machine, directed by Josef Goebbels, excelled itself. The SA crossed the country in lorries to march and countermarch in enormous demonstrations. Nazi leaders toured Germany to the accompaniment of torchlight processions and mass meetings. It was a performance none of Hitler's rivals could match, although Hindenburg's supporters were by no means passive. Brüning, touring the country in the President's stead, revealed himself as a speaker of force and sincerity, even if he lacked the arts of a demagogue. The Social Democrats had already set up what they called an 'Iron Front' to defend democracy. Based largely on the Social Democratic party and the Reichsbanner it now tried to rally Republican forces behind the President.

* It should be mentioned that business funds found their way into the coffers of most German parties – it being considered useful for industrial interests to have links with any group which might become politically powerful.

Hindenburg won the election, but was forced to go through a second round of voting because he did not gain an overall majority on the first ballot. Hitler received well over thirteen million votes. It was clear that the 'National opposition' to the Weimar Republic had at last found an effective leader. Roughly speaking, the basis of Hitler's support lay in the middle classes and the farming communities of Protestant Germany. Hindenburg owed his re-election largely to the Social Democratic working class and the Roman Catholics.

This was not a result to please either the President or the Reichswehr. It reinforced the charge made by Hindenburg's Nationalist critics that he had sold himself to the anti-German forces of Marxism and the Pope. Brüning was the man held responsible in the President's entourage for having put the old field-marshal in such a false position.

It should be stressed that at this time there was no reason why Hitler should have been regarded as an invincible force in German politics. Indeed, the nation had, by its votes, shown that it rejected dictatorship from the left or the right. Had the President and the army leaders been determined to defeat Hitler they could easily have done so. There were plenty of loyal Republicans ready to help them. The Reichsbanner had been organising defence units to supplement the police in the event of a *coup* by the SA. Braun, the Prussian Prime Minister, whose state's police were a thorn in the flesh of Nazi and Communist trouble-makers, suggested on several occasions that there should be a consolidation of Reich and Prussian authorities in Berlin. This would have strengthened the forces loyal to the constitution and identified the Social Democrats quite clearly with the Reich government.[16]

Von Schleicher and his friends wanted none of this. They were furious when the Social Democrats tried to present themselves as allies of the State. On 25 March Schleicher wrote to Groener complaining that the socialists were trying to associate him with their activities. Referring to the date of the second presidential ballot, he went on:

I am really looking forward to 11 April – then it will be possible to talk to this lying brood with no holds barred. . . . After the events of the last days I am really glad that there is a counterweight [to the Social Democrats] in the form of the Nazis, who are not very decent chaps either and must be stomached with the greatest caution. If they did not exist, we should virtually have to invent them.[17]

The victim of all this spleen was to be Chancellor Brüning.

Hindenburg, whose age was a serious handicap to his judgement, was told on all sides that Brüning had lost public confidence. He was disturbed when the Government drew up plans for a very moderate land reform in eastern Germany. These involved breaking up some of the more spectacularly bankrupt estates and making them available as small-holdings to the unemployed. It was denounced as 'agrarian bolshevism' by the landed interest. Meanwhile von Schleicher had become convinced that he could win Nazi agreement to support a right-wing government. In return they would have to be granted new Reichstag elections and the repeal of a ban on the SA which Brüning's government had finally imposed after a long period of violence and provocation.

On 30 May Brüning was dismissed from office by Hindenburg. His replacement was Franz von Papen, a protégé of von Schleicher who lacked political experience and parliamentary support. The way was clear for Hitler to take another step in his bid for power.

Brüning's fall was a real turning-point in the collapse of German democracy. Until then the rising Nazi tides had been contained. Now they could burst forth in a menacing flood. The fate of Germany was in the hands of General von Schleicher, who left the comparative obscurity of his military office and entered the new cabinet as Defence Minister.

Von Schleicher and von Papen had a plan of campaign
according to which they would dissolve the Reichstag, raise
the ban on the SA and eliminate the socialist-dominated
government in Prussia. They believed that these measures
would encourage the Nazis to support the régime. On the
diplomatic front, concessions wrung from the forthcoming
disarmament conference would – it was hoped – enable the
Government to create a reserve military force into which the
nationalist energies of the nation's youth could be channelled
with safety.

The hopes pinned on 'taming' the Nazis proved vain.
Hitler showed no gratitude when the Government, having
dissolved the Reichstag, lifted the ban on the SA and forced
Land authorities to give up their own local restrictions.[18]
On the contrary, having obtained their concessions the Nazis
became rapidly more obstreperous. Nevertheless, von
Papen pressed on with his action to destroy the Republican
régime in Prussia. He saw this as a move to consolidate the
power of the central government and to pave the way for a
more authoritarian type of system in Germany, untram-
melled by the rights of federal states.

Otto Braun's cabinet in Prussia was a vulnerable target.
Landtag elections in April had destroyed its parliamentary
support. The lifting of the ban on Hitler's storm-troopers
caused an immediate and alarming upsurge of violence.
Murderous encounters took place, especially between Nazis
and Communists. Deaths were frequent. Von Papen's own
government was entirely responsible for this, but he
preferred to blame that of Prussia. On 20 July he suppressed it, acting on presidential authority.

Politically von Papen's daring did him nothing but harm.
The Nazis and the Communists were delighted; one of the
main bulwarks of Weimar democracy had been destroyed.
The Social Democrats and Centre were indignant at the
removal of their ministers. Governments in other large
German states like Bavaria and Württemberg were seriously

alarmed lest the same fate should befall them. In Prussia itself the Social Democrats had toyed with the idea of resistance. Many of the rank and file in the party, the Reichsbanner and the trade unions were bewildered and angry when their leaders surrendered to von Papen. The younger Social Democrats who formed the backbone of the Reichsbanner Defence Units (*Schufos*) had been eager to fight. It was also suggested that the Prussian police might be used to defend their own government.

Yet the leaders of the 'Iron Front' – including the Social Democratic ministers, the trade union officials and the Reichsbanner commanders – all had to agree that no effective resistance was possible.[19] There were more than 200,000 men in the *Schufos*, but they had had no proper military training or equipment. Against the Reichswehr, doubtless supported by the SA and the Stahlhelm, they could have had no chance. Even on moral grounds there was some doubt about their position. They would have been fighting for a government which had been defeated at the polls. Against them was ranged a presidential authority recently confirmed by massive popular vote.

It is certainly true that the Social Democratic Party and the 'Iron Front' had never prepared themselves for a civil war in which they would be the revolutionary factor. They were used to operating within the framework of the law, and when that framework began to collapse around them they lacked the ability to improvise resistance. The Social Democratic ministers in Prussia have been criticised for taking no steps to fight for survival after von Papen came to power, even though his intentions were clear. It is difficult to see exactly what could have been done. Von Papen did not take office until May, by which time the Prussian government was operating on a caretaker basis with no majority. To have organised Prussia for civil war while Brüning was Chancellor would have been criminally irresponsible.[20] In 1932 the Social Democratic Party had more members than in 1928. Many of its supporters would have been ready to fight to save German democracy. That they could not do so was only partly due to the weakness of their own leadership. Their real mistake lay in trusting Hindenburg to defend the constitution.

And if they had not?

On 31 July the Reichstag elections took place. As had been expected, they were a triumph for Hitler. His party received 13·7 million votes – 330,000 more than in the second ballot of the presidential elections four months previously. The Nazis had 230 seats in the Reichstag – by far the largest number ever attained by a single party. Their share of the poll was 37·4 per cent. They were the strongest party in all Protestant German electoral districts except Berlin, and in many of mixed religious character also.[21] Only the proportional representation system had prevented them from obtaining an absolute majority in parliament.

Von Papen's government had no cause to be happy with the results. The Chancellor had not been associated with any particular party, but the German Nationalists, the People's Party and the Nationalist splinter groups which had broken from Hugenberg were sympathetic towards his régime. Of these the Nationalists nearly held their ground, but still lost 300,000 votes. They returned 37 deputies to the Reichstag. The People's Party and the smaller groups suffered a complete disaster. Their eagerness to appease anti-democratic and nationalist sentiment simply encouraged their supporters to go the whole hog and vote for Hitler. The Social Democrats and the Centre, who had openly opposed von Papen and the Nazis, fared better. The fact that the Communist Party polled more than five million votes scarcely made von Papen's position any more secure.

The only possible coalition in the new Reichstag seemed to be between the Nazis and the Centre Party. Together they would have commanded a majority. Negotiations took place between them but led to no result. Hitler was determined to receive the Chancellorship and wreak his vengeance on the 'Marxists'. President Hindenburg, on the other hand, set his face against both Hitler and a cabinet based on parliament. If the Nazis entered the Government it would be as subordinates in a presidential régime. During these months Hitler showed great political courage in refusing anything but the highest post. There were important men in his party, the most prominent being Gregor Strasser, who felt that the Nazi wave had reached its crest and that the time had come to taste the fruits of office. There was reason in this. Hitler's intransigence was beginning to alarm some of his wealthy business patrons. They found von Papen, who was sympathetic to industrial interests, more attractive than earlier Chancellors, and they detected ominous signs of social radicalism in the SA. Some of them cut their links with the Nazis and others became less generous.[22] In the party as a whole the frenzied activism of the previous months could not be maintained without tangible achievements.

The danger to the Nazis was demonstrated in the autumn of 1932 when von Papen, faced with a completely unco-operative Reichstag, dissolved it yet again. On 6 November Germans trooped to the polls once more. Electoral participation was still high, although not the astonishing 83 per cent registered in July. For the first time since 1928 the Nazis lost votes in a Reichstag election, their share of the poll falling from 37·4 per cent to 33·1 per cent. The German Nationalists, who had begun to stress their difference with the Nazis, gained nearly 800,000 votes, and the People's Party improved its position slightly, though it only returned eleven deputies. Von Papen could claim that he was making ground, despite the fact that his supporters were still a tiny minority. He and President Hindenburg were quite prepared to go on governing without parliament – a breach of the constitution – until they were ready to implement a complete programme of constitutional reform. Von Papen had drawn up a number of public works schemes which he hoped would ease the unemployment situation. If the army and the President kept their trust in him he might survive.

It was here that von Papen's political inexperience revealed itself. His unpopularity was so widespread that even his colleagues feared a civil war if the Government openly violated the constitution on his behalf. Such fears had been increased at the beginning of November, when Nazis and Communists had collaborated to organise a transport strike in Berlin. Acts of sabotage and violence accompanied this extremist alliance. Upbraided by his wealthier sympathisers, Hitler replied that, unless he allowed his rank and file to take such action, they would desert to the Communists. Reichswehr commanders were alarmed lest their soldiers should have to fight the SA and the Communists. They thought the Poles might take the opportunity to attack Germany. Their anxiety was almost certainly exaggerated. A partnership between Nazis and Communists would have been difficult to maintain and would have aroused fierce opposition from such disparate political elements as the Reichsbanner and the Stahlhelm. Nevertheless, von Schleicher, now convinced that von Papen was a liability, stressed the dark side of the military picture, and his cabinet colleagues agreed with him. Von Papen resigned.

On 2 December von Schleicher himself became Chancellor. It was an exposed position which he had not coveted. Power without responsibility had been his goal. In one important respect he was even weaker than von Papen. His relations with the President had grown cooler since the previous spring. Von Papen had quite replaced him in Hindenburg's favour.[23]

Von Schleicher was an ingenious man who did not lack courage. Having failed once more to negotiate with Hitler, he attempted to create popular support for his government by cutting across normal party lines. Gregor Strasser, still regarded as Hitler's main rival within the Nazi Party, had previously indicated that he might be willing to break with his chief and take office under another Chancellor. Von Schleicher also tried to appeal to the trade unions with schemes of work creation. He envisaged projects for compulsory youth training and cheap labour for farmers. Had he remained in office, he was even prepared to consider nationalising the coal and steel industry.[24]

Imaginative though these ideas were, they quickly collapsed in practice. Strasser was forced to resign his offices in the Nazi Party on 8 December. The Christian and Social Democratic Trade Unions rebuffed von Schleicher. In desperation he turned to the Social Democrats but, fortified with the belief that the Nazi tide had turned, they refused to join his government. Schleicher was forced to ask Hindenburg for the power to govern unconstitutionally – something which had been refused to von Papen.

The President had no desire to accept this. Besides, it was not necessary. Von Papen had been negotiating with Hitler, and had convinced Hindenburg that the Nazi leader should be given the post of Chancellor. Von Papen was confident he could control Hitler. Schleicher had to resign. He greatly feared that Papen would be his successor. The Reichswehr leaders thought that this really would lead to a civil war in which 90 per cent of the nation would be against them. Their apprehension soon disappeared. On 30 January Hitler became Reich Chancellor.

His appointment was quite unnecessary. His coalition government, in which Hugenberg's Nationalists were the only other party represented, had no majority in the Reichstag. The Nazis could not have threatened the State if they had been denied power. Their movement was waning. A further period of frustration might have finished them off. It was perhaps for this reason that Hitler became attractive to men of property in Germany. If his mass support ebbed away the beneficiaries would either be the democratic Weimar parties or the Communists. The dream of national resurgence based on an authoritarian régime would then have been destroyed.

In any case, von Papen and his friends thought they could manage the Nazis. Hitler's men had only two major posts in the Reich government, those of the Chancellor and Minister of the Interior. Von Papen was Vice-Chancellor and Prime Minister of Prussia, and had the ear of the President. A general, Blomberg, headed the Defence Ministry. Hugenberg was Minister of Economics and Food, and Seldte, the Stahlhelm leader, Minister of Labour. There seemed little danger that the Nazis would overwhelm their colleagues.

Within a month Hitler had demonstrated how complacent von Papen had been. Having made a show of negotiating for a coalition with the Centre, Hitler persuaded his colleagues to dissolve the Reichstag for a third general election. He promised them that he would not change the complexion of his cabinet even if he won. The election campaign was conducted under quite unfair conditions, because the authority of the state was at Hitler's disposal. Göring had been appointed Prussian Minister of the Interior, and thus controlled police power in almost two-thirds of Germany. He recruited 50,000 'auxiliary police', most of whom were Nazi storm-troopers. The regular police were purged and ordered to protect Nazis and Nationalists against 'Marxist' attack.

On 27 February the Reichstag in Berlin was set on fire by a young Dutchman of extreme left-wing opinions. Using this as a pretext to claim that Germany was threatened by a Bolshevik *coup*, Hitler issued a presidential decree 'for the Protection of the People and the State'. For many years this was to be one of the main foundations of Nazi tyranny. It swept away constitutional safeguards against arbitrary arrest and the suppression of free speech.[25] A wave of arrests followed. Hitler's opponents believed that the Reichstag fire had been a Nazi plot. This now seems unlikely, but the issue is not an important one. The Nazis had made preparations to take emergency action before the fire, and, had it not occurred, other excuses would have been found.[26]

The Reichstag elections on 5 April did not give Hitler an absolute majority, despite the enormous pressure exerted on the electorate. But with almost 44 per cent of the vote, and in coalition with Hugenberg's Nationalists, Hitler could command a simple majority in the Reichstag. The opposition to him was completely incapable of offering effective resistance. The Centre Party had already shown itself willing to collaborate with Hitler, and its leader, prelate Kaas, now desired only to safeguard the religious freedom of German Catholics.[27] The parties of the moderate right had already been destroyed as an electoral force in the summer of 1932. The Communists were arrested or forced into hiding. Only the Social Democrats tried to put a brave face on defeat. When, on 23 March 1933, Hitler presented the Reichstag with an enabling law empowering him to rule by decree, the Social Democrats were the one group to vote against it. With that last gesture of defiance, their Weimar Republic was finally interred. Hitler was the master of Germany.

Hitler had exploited his chances with great skill. Yet he had been remarkably fortunate in the turn of events since 1929. Under the pressure of the economic crisis parliament virtually abdicated responsibility for the nation's affairs to a Chancellor ruling with the support of the President and the army. Brüning's decision to call a Reichstag election in 1930 gave Hitler the opportunity to demonstrate his mass appeal, and rendered the re-establishment of parliamentary government virtually impossible. This left the Republic dependent upon a military, bureaucratic and business establishment which had no emotional loyalty towards it.

Such a régime could not arouse mass enthusiasm in Germany. It deliberately refrained from associating itself with militant Republican elements such as the Reichsbanner. The '*Parteihader*' (party squabbles) of the Weimar system were regarded with distaste, even by those who did not wish to act unconstitutionally. Brüning hoped for a limited monarchy, and von Papen for a corporate State dominated by the propertied classes. Von Schleicher had dreams of a national concentration headed by the army, in which organised Labour would participate and political parties disappear. It is difficult to see how – even if Hitler had not been called to power – the Weimar Republic could have reverted to its former democratic system.

The failure of German democracy after the First World War cannot be attributed to any single cause. Three explanations are commonly given: that the German revolution was not sweeping enough and did not create institutions loyal to the new régime; that the Versailles Peace Treaty saddled the Republic with impossible burdens; and that the Weimar Constitution was impracticable.

The first of these explanations has some force, but it remains difficult to envisage what form a really radical revolution in Germany would have taken. Only the most extreme elements in the labour movement could have carried it through in 1919, and, as events showed, they lacked mass support. So far as the peace treaty is concerned, its demoralising impact on German public opinion was more important than its physical effects. Within ten years of the treaty Germany seemed to have made a remarkable economic recovery, and her international standing was being restored under Stresemann's guidance. Doubtless the financial aspects of the peace settlement contributed to the economic disaster which overwhelmed Germany from 1929 to 1933. But other countries – among them many of the victor powers – experienced an almost equally catastrophic recession. As for the constitution, it is difficult to see how any parliamentary system can be made proof against the electorate.

The Republic was never able to build up a stable block

of parliamentary supporters. There is no doubt that it inherited many political weaknesses from the old Wilhelmine Empire. The Reichstag parties showed little enthusiasm for the acceptance of government responsibility. They remained closely associated with sectional or class interests. It was particularly unfortunate that no powerful Republican party appeared which could appeal to Germany's Protestant middle class. German liberalism had been divided and demoralised in the era of Bismarck and Wilhelm II. It was never able to consolidate itself under the Republic.

The parties which adapted best to the new situation were those representing the social outsiders in the German Empire – the Roman Catholic Centre and the Social Democrats. This increased the resentment of those who had felt themselves to be the backbone of the nation before 1918. In particular, the Social Democrats were pictured as revolutionaries, and their spokesmen sometimes encouraged this impression by talking in terms of class war. Fear of 'Marxism' was increased by the disturbances – the extent of which was commonly exaggerated – in the November revolution. It grew stronger after the humiliation of the peace treaty and the very real hardships caused by inflation. When the economic depression created an atmosphere of internal crisis the bourgeois parties lost their voters to Hitler, while the Roman Catholic Centre and the Social Democrats put up far stiffer resistance to the Nazi challenge.

Germany's political problems were exacerbated by the conflict of generations after 1918. The older parties appeared to have learned nothing from the experience of the war. In the SPD, trade union and party functionaries seemed concerned with problems more relevant to 1914 than to the 1920s. The same was true of the socially superior leadership of the German Nationalist Party. The youth of the country was frustrated both intellectually and professionally by this age bottleneck, and herein lay one of the most effective appeals of the Nazi and Communist parties. Youth – rather than totalitarianism – was their most striking common factor. It was this youthful dynamism which made the Nazis attractive to the army and the former ruling classes of the Wilhelmine Empire. They hoped to use it to restore the type of political supremacy they had enjoyed in Germany before 1914. Many went on to prosper in the Third Reich. Others quickly realised how grievously they had been mistaken.

[1] Bullock, *Hitler*, p. 115.

[2] See Hale, *The Captive Press*, pp. 27–8 and *passim*.

[3] For the various versions of *Mein Kampf*, see Hammer, 'Die deutschen Ausgaben von Hitlers "Mein Kampf"', pp. 161–78. Also Maser, *Hitlers 'Mein Kampf'* (Munich, Bechtle, 1966) pp. 69–70.

This is not the place to discuss Hitler's foreign policy aims as set out in *Mein Kampf* and elsewhere. Hitler's ideas were certainly affected by circumstances, as are those of all politicians. Nevertheless, the remarkable coincidence of his published thoughts and his later achievements can hardly be overlooked. For conflicting views on this subject, see Trevor-Roper, 'Hitlers Kriegsziele' and Taylor, *The Origins of the Second World War*, pp. 22–3, 98. Very illuminating on Hitler's intentions in the 1930s is Robertson, *Hitler's Pre-war Policy and Plans* (London, 1963).

[4] For accounts of Hitler's policy at this time see Bullock, *Hitler*, pp. 130–40 and Noakes, 'Conflict and Development in the NSDAP 1924–27'.

[5] Milatz, *Wähler und Wahlen*, pp. 112, 125–6.

[6] Rohe, *Reichsbanner*, pp. 360–5.

[7] Dorpalen, *Hindenburg*, p. 207; Bracher, *Auflösung*, pp. 370–1.

[8] Berghahn, *Stahlhelm*, pp. 155 ff.

[9] Born, *Bankenkrise*, p. 53.

[10] Ibid. p. 54. The commentator was Lujo Brentano.

[11] See, for example, Schorr, *Adam Stegerwald*, pp. 188–9. Stegerwald was Minister of Labour and a Catholic Trade Unionist.

[12] Bennet, *Germany and the Financial Crisis*, pp. 11–12.

[13] Ibid. p. 306.

[14] See Brüning, 'Ein Brief', pp. 10–11.

[15] Bullock, *Hitler*, pp. 196–9.

[16] Braun, *Von Weimar zu Hitler*, p. 277.

[17] Carsten, *Reichswehr*, pp. 339–40.

[18] Bracher, *Auflösung*, pp. 545–52; Vogelsang, *Reichswehr*, p. 221.

[19] Rohe, *Reichsbanner*, p. 431. Höltermann, the Reichsbanner leader, favoured resistance as a gesture, but accepted the judgement of his Reichsbanner colleagues that the situation was hopeless.

[20] For a discussion of these problems, see Matthias–Morsey, *Ende der Parteien*, pp. 127–45 and Rohe, *Reichsbanner*, pp. 432–5.

[21] Milatz, *Wähler und Wahlen*, p. 142.

[22] Dorpalen, *Hindenburg*, p. 365. Also Treue, 'Der deutsche Unternehmer in der Weltwirtschaftskrise 1928–33', in *Staats- und Wirtschaftskrise* (eds. Conze–Raupach), pp. 123–4.

[23] Dorpalen, *Hindenburg*, pp. 395–7.

[24] Vorgelsang, *Reichswehr*, pp. 346–9, 381.

[25] Bullock, *Hitler*, p. 263.

[26] Bracher–Sauer–Schulz, *Machtergreifung*, p. 82.

[27] Aretin, 'Prälat Kaas, Franz von Papen und das Reichskonkordat von 1933', pp. 254–79.

For the Centre attitude see Matthias–Morsey, *Ende der Parteien*, pp. 355–67. Many Centre Party members feared a new *Kulturkampf* if they voted against the law.

Chronological Table

1918	28/29 September	The German High Command advises the Kaiser to establish a parliamentary cabinet and sue for peace
	1 October	Prince Max of Baden appointed Chancellor
	23 October	President Wilson's Third Note implying that peace could not be negotiated unless the Kaiser abdicates
	28 October	Naval mutinies begin in Kiel
	7/8 November	Bavarian monarchy overthrown and a Republic declared in Munich
	9 November	Republic declared in Berlin. Ebert heads first Republican government – a coalition of Majority and Independent Social Democrats The Kaiser flees to Holland
	11 November	Erzberger concludes an armistice with Marshal Foch
	16–20 December	Congress of Workers' and Soldiers' Councils in Berlin. Votes to hold elections for a National Assembly
	27 December	Independent Social Democrats leave the Government
	31 December	Foundation of the German Communist Party in Berlin
1919	5–12 January	Spartakist rising in Berlin
	15 January	Rosa Luxemburg and Karl Liebknecht murdered by government forces
	19 January	Elections for the National Assembly
	6 February	National Assembly meets at Weimar

	7 April	Bavarian Soviet Republic proclaimed in Munich
	1 May	Bavarian Soviet suppressed by Reichswehr and Bavarian Freikorps
	28 June	Treaty of Versailles signed
	11 August	The Constitution of the German Republic formally promulgated
	21 August	Friedrich Ebert takes the oath as President
	September	Hitler joins the German Workers' Party in Munich
1920	24 February	Hitler announces new programme of the National Socialist German Workers Party (formally German Workers' Party)
	13 March	Kapp Putsch. Ebert and ministers flee to Stuttgart
	17 March	Collapse of Putsch
	24 March	Defence Minister Noske and army chief Reinhardt resign. Gessler and von Seeckt take their places
	6 June	1st Reichstag election. SPD wins 102 seats; USPD 84; DNVP 71; DVP 65; Centre 64; DDP 39; BVP 21; KPD 4
	5–16 July	International Conference at Spa
1921	21 March	Plebiscite in Upper Silesia
	27 April	Reparations Commission sets German debt at 132 thousand million gold marks
	5 May	Allied ultimatum delivered in London requiring German compliance with conditions about disarmament, reparations and war criminals
	26–29 July	Hitler becomes undisputed leader of the Nazis
	26 August	Erzberger assassinated
1922	16 April	German–Soviet Agreement signed at Rapallo

	24 June	Assassination of Rathenau
	18 July	'Law to Protect the Republic' passed by the Reichstag
1923	10 January	Germany declared in default on reparations payments
	11/12 January	Franco-Belgian forces occupy the Ruhr and the German government declares passive resistance
	Summer 1923	Inflation of currency completely out of control
	13 August	Stresemann becomes Chancellor
	26 September	Passive resistance ended. Von Kahr declares state of emergency in Bavaria and establishes himself as State Commissioner
	27 September	Ebert declares state of emergency throughout Germany. Gessler given full powers under Article 48 of Constitution
	1–3 October	Buchrucker Putsch suppressed at Kustrin
	29 October	Socialist/Communist governments suppressed in Saxony and Thuringia
	2 November	SPD ministers in Berlin resign
	8/9 November	Hitler Putsch in Munich
	15 November	First Rentenmark notes issued
	23 November	Stresemann resigns as Chancellor but continues to serve as Foreign Minister
1924	13 February	President Ebert declares end of state of emergency
	1 April	Hitler sentenced to five years fortress arrest
	4 May	2nd Reichstag election. SPD 100; DNVP 95; Centre 65; KPD 62; DVP 45; Racialists 32; DDP 28; BVP 16; Landbund 10; Economics Party 10

	9 August	London Conference protocol accepting the Dawes Plan for reparations payments
	7 December	3rd Reichstag election. SPD 131; DNVP 103; Centre 69; DVP 51; KPD 45; DDP 32; BVP 19; Economics Party 17; Racialists 14; Landbund 8
1925	28 February	President Ebert dies
	27 April	Hindenburg elected President
	5 October	Locarno Treaty initialled
1926	24 April	German–Soviet Non-aggression pact
	8 September	Germany elected to the League of Nations
	9 October	Von Seeckt resigns as head of the Reichswehr. Succeeded by Heye
1927	31 January	Allied Control Commission withdrawn from Germany
1928	30 January	Defence Minister Gessler resigns. Groener becomes Minister of Defence
	20 May	4th Reichstag election. SPD 153; Centre 62; DNVP 73; KPD 54; DVP 24; DDP 25; Economics Party 23; BVP 16; Nazis 12; Landvolk 10; Farmers' Party 8; Landbund 3
1929	7 June	Young Plan drawn up in Paris
	6–31 August	First Hague Conference on Young Plan. Agreement on evacuation of Rhineland
	3 October	Stresemann dies
1930	30 March	Brüning appointed Reich Chancellor
	14 September	5th Reichstag Election. SPD 143; Nazis 107; KPD 77; Centre 68; DNVP 41; DVP 30; Economics Party 23; DDP 20; BVP 19; Landvolk 19; German Farmers' Party 6; Landbund 3

1931	20 June	President Hoover suggests Moratorium on reparations and War Debts
	13–14 July	DANAT Bank closes its doors. 'Bank holiday' in Germany
1932	10 April	Hindenburg re-elected President
	13 April	SA and other Nazi para-military formations suppressed
	13 May	Groener resigns post as Defence Minister
	30 May	Brüning resigns. Von Papen Chancellor
	16 June– 9 July	Lausanne Conference on reparations
	17 June	Ban on SA lifted
	20 July	Von Papen deposes Prussian government
	31 July	6th Reichstag election. Nazis 230; SPD 133; KPD 89; Centre 75; DNVP 37; BVP 22; DVP 7; DDP 4; Economics Party 2
	6 November	7th Reichstag election. Nazis 196; SPD 121; KPD 100; Centre 70; DNVP 52; BVP 20; DVP 11
	17 November	Von Papen resigns
	2 December	Von Schleicher appointed Chancellor
1933	28 January	Von Schleicher resigns
	30 January	Hitler appointed Chancellor
	27 February	Reichstag fire
	28 February	Decree to Protect the German People and the State
	5 March	8th Reichstag election. Nazis 288; SPD 120; KPD 81; Centre 74; DNVP 52; BVP 18; DVP 2
	23 March	Enabling Act passed through Reichstag

Bibliography

SCHOLARS of German history are fortunate in the availability of a large variety of sources, and in particular of official documents captured by the Allies at the end of the Second World War. Many of these – including most of the records of the German Foreign Office – are available on microfilm. Publication of the series of German diplomatic documents covering the Weimar period has now begun, although attention naturally centred first on those documents which dealt with the period leading up to the Second World War.

On the collapse of the Empire and the German Revolution the books by Professor E. Matthias and Professors Matthias and Morsey contain sources of great value for the light they cast on the reform movement in the German Reichstag before November 1918. These are:

E. MATTHIAS, *Der Interfraktionelle Ausschuss 1917–1918*, 2 vols. (Düsseldorf, Droste, 1959).

E. MATTHIAS and R. MORSEY, *Die Regierung des Prinzen Max von Baden* (Düsseldorf, Droste, 1962).

The memoirs of Prince Max von Baden should still be consulted, as should Arnold Brecht's fascinating autobiography, which adds to our knowledge of the confused and difficult situation in the Chancellery on the eve of revolution. The most recent account of the German Revolution to appear in English is that by Dr A. J. Ryder. It is a balanced and sensible assessment and deals especially well with the wealth of memoir material – much of it polemical – on the revolutionary side.

The flavour of the revolution and the success of Majority Socialist attempts to moderate it comes out well from C. B. Burdick's and R. H. Lutz's *The Political Institutions of the German Empire*, a book of documents on the revolutionary period which, though very selective, has yet to find a more comprehensive counterpart in German.

Probably the most illuminating book to appear on the German Revolution in recent years is Eberhard Kolb's history of the Workers' Councils.

On the Foundations of the Republic Professor Bracher's early chapters in *Die Auflösung der Weimarer Republik* and his general reflections in *Deutschland zwischen Monarchie und Diktatur* deal very effectively with the problems presented by the Weimar constitution, and by the nature of Germany's civil service, political parties and officer corps. On the important question of the reform of the bureaucratic system in Prussia, Wolfgang Runge's *Beamtentum im Parteienstaat* gives a good picture of the extent to which the Prussian civil service was Republicanised and the difficulties faced by reforming ministers in achieving this end.

On the army there is a very large bibliography, but Professor Carsten's recent history of the Reichswehr is quite outstanding. Sir John Wheeler-Bennett's *Nemesis of Power* remains a classic indictment of military interference in German politics, and its main conclusions have been reinforced by the documentary evidence which has appeared since it was written. Important information on the organisation of secret reserve formations in Prussia, as well as on the political ideas of General Schleicher, are to be found in Thilo Vogelsang's *Reichswehr, Staat und NSDAP*. Herr Hans Meier-Welcker's biography of Seeckt contains much interesting detail.

So far as political parties are concerned the German Social Democratic Party still lacks a definitive history, as indeed, do most of its rivals. Professor Hunt's *German Social Democracy* is a useful survey. The most important book to appear on a single party is Professor Morsey's analysis of the Centre, but this only takes the story up to 1923. The origins of the German People's Party are described by W. Hartenstein in *Die Anfänge der deutschen Volkspartei*, but perhaps the best picture of the Party in action is in Turner's *Stresemann and the Politics of the Weimar Republic*. A good idea of the tensions within the German National People's Party emerges from Hertzmann's *DNVP*, but much more work needs to be done on this subject. The extreme left has fared badly from the historiographical viewpoint, although a great deal of detailed work is being conducted at the moment. Neither Prager's history of the Independent Social Democrats nor Flechtheim's work on the KPD can be regarded as very much more than political testaments. The early years of the Communist Party have, however, received a detailed and balanced treatment from Werner Angress in his *Stillborn Revolution*.

Two of the para-military formations which played such an important part in Republican political life have received illuminating and scholarly treatment in Karl Rohe's *Reichs-banner* and Volker Berghann's *Stahlhelm*. The Nazi Party can best be understood by reading about its real creator in Alan Bullock's *Hitler, a Study in Tyranny*. Werner Maser's *Frühgeschichte* gives an interesting and detailed account of the party's early struggles in Bavaria, but does not alter the main outlines of Bullock's account. The best short description of the nature of National Socialism is Martin Broszat's *Der Nationalsozialismus*.

On the making of Peace 1918–19 Alma Luckau's *The German Delegation at the Peace Conference* remains very important though sadly difficult to obtain. Klaus Epstein's biography of Erzberger is informative on the armistice and the critical negotiations leading up to the German acceptance of the Versailles Treaty. German attempts to stress the transformed nature of German politics in order to attract the *Entente* are illustrated in H. Holborn's article in *The Diplomats*. The extent of their failure can be read in vol. XII of *Foreign Relations of the United States. The Paris Peace Conference*. German–Russian relations are particularly well served for the early part of the Republic's history by G. Freund, *Unholy Alliance*. The military relationships are set out in Professor Carsten's *Reichswehr*.

The collapse of the Republic is best studied in Professor Bracher's *Auflösung der Weimarer Republik* and *National-sozialistische Machtergreifung*. The volume on the demise of

Germany's political parties, *Das Ende der Parteien* by Professors Matthias and Morsey, is also essential. Professor Conze has some challenging comments on the Brüning government in his chapter in *Die Staats- und Wirtschaftskrise das deutschen Reiches*, while E. W. Bennett presents a critical picture of Brüning's foreign policy in *Germany and the Diplomacy of the Financial Crisis* (Harvard U.P., 1962). On the crisis itself a fascinating picture of German financial problems and the Government's attempts to deal with them is provided in Dr Born's book on the weaknessses of the German banking system. R. E. Luke's *Von der Stabilisierung zur Krise* is important for the relationship between Germany's reparation problem and her economic difficulties in the depression.

The victory of National Socialism has attracted many writers, but mention should be made of three local studies which throw light on the nature of the support for Hitler. The most impressive is Heberle's analysis of Nazi growth among the farming communities of Schleswig-Holstein. Roloff's description of the Nazi victory in Brunswick illustrates the stages by which bourgeois parties lost their voters to the Nazis. W. S. Allen stresses the conflict between classes in his study of a small town in the Weser Valley.

On the whole question of elections and electoral movements Milatz's study *Wähler und Wahlen in der Weimarer Republik* is invaluable.

Leading figures in the Republic have not been fortunate in their biographers. Kotowski's biography of Ebert stops at the end of the First World War. Rathenau has been sensitively and sympathetically treated by Count Harry Kessler, and Mr Joll. Andreas Dorpalen's political biography of Hindenburg is a most useful and thoughtful book. The best treatment of all has been reserved for Hitler: Alan Bullock's picture of him remains unsurpassed.

Books mentioned in this brief survey, and others of particular importance, are marked with an asterisk. The place of publication is London unless otherwise stated.

The best general history of the Weimar Republic in English is:

ERICH EYCK, *A History of the Weimar Republic*, 2 vols., tr. H. P. Hanson and R. G. L. Waite (Harvard and Oxford U.P., 1962 and 1964).

This is especially good when dealing with parliamentary politics, foreign policy and constitutional questions. Social and economic questions are given less detailed consideration, although Eyck still has a good many sensible things to say about them.

Still required reading are:

ARTHUR ROSENBERG, *The Birth of the German Republic* (O.U.P., 1931).
— *A History of the German Republic* (Methuen, 1936).

The following list of books and articles is selective. For more detailed information the reader is referred to the following:

DAHLMANN–WAITZ, *Quellenkunde der deutschen Geschichte. Bibliographie der Quellen und der Literatur der deutschen Geschichte*, 10 ed. book 8, section 393–4 (Stuttgart, Anton Hiersemann, 1965).
BRUNO GEBHARDT, *Handbuch der deutschen Geschichte*, 8th ed. vol. 4 (Stuttgart, Union Verlag, 1959).
BRANDT–MEYER–JUST, *Handbuch der deutschen Geschichte*, vol. IV, section 3, 'Die Weimarer Republik' (1958).
section 4, 'Die Diktatur Hitlers bis zum Beginn des zweiten Weltkrieges' (1961).
Wiener Library. Catalogue Series No. 2. *From Weimar to Hitler, Germany 1918–1933* (Vallentine, Mitchell, 1964).

The bibliographical appendices published in the *Vierteljahrshefte für Zeitgeschichte* should also be consulted.

I. PUBLICATIONS OF DOCUMENTS AND OTHER SOURCE MATERIALS

C. B. BURDICK and R. H. LUTZ, *The Political Institutions of the German Revolution* (Stanford U.P. and London, 1966).

J. HOHLFELD (ed.), *Dokumente der deutschen Politik und Geschichte vom 1948 bis zur Gegenwart* (Berlin, Dokumentem-Verlag/Dr Herbert Wendler, 1951–).

HÖLFRON, *Die deutsche Nationalversammlung im Jahre 1919* (Berlin, 1919).

P. MANTOUX, *Les Deliberations du Conseil des Quatre* (Paris, Editions du Centre National de la Recherche Scientifique, 1955).

E. MATTHIAS, *Der Interfraktionelle Ausschuss 1917–1918*, 2 vols. (Düsseldorf, Droste, 1959).

E. MATTHIAS and R. MORSEY, *Die Regierung des Prinzen Max von Baden* (Düsseldorf, Droste, 1962).

H. MICHAELIS, E. SCHRAEPLER and G. SCHEEL, *Ursachen und Folgen. Vom deutschen Zusammenbruch 1918 und 1945 bis zur staatlichen Neuordnung Deutschlands in der Gegenwart* (Berlin, Dokumenten-Verlag, 1958–).

H. ROTHFELS, M. BEAUMONT, A. BULLOCK and H. M. SMYTHE (eds.), Akten zur deutschen auswärtigen Politik 1918–1945, Series B, 1925–1945, vol. I, 1 (Göttingen, Vandenhoeck & Rupprecht, 1966).

LEO STERN, *Die Auswirkungen der grossen sozialistischen Oktoberrevolution auf Deutschland*, 4 vols. (E. Berlin, Rütten und Loening, 1959).

2. BIOGRAPHIES, MEMOIRS, DIARIES AND WORKS CONTAINING SOURCE MATERIALS

*PRINZ MAX VON BADEN, *Erinnerungen und Dokumente* (Stuttgart, DVA, 1927).

EMIL BARTH, *Aus der Werkstatt der deutschen Revolution* (Berlin, Hoffmann, 1919).

*OTTO BRAUN, *Von Weimar zu Hitler* (Hamburg, Norddeutsche Verlagsanstalt, 1949).

*ARNOLD BRECHT, *Aus nächster Nähe. Lebenserinnerungen eines beteiligten Beobachters 1884–1927* (Stuttgart, DVA, 1966).

U. VON BROCKDORFF-RANTZAU, *Dokumente und Gedanken um Versailles* (Berlin, Verlag für Kulturpolitik, 1925).

*KLAUS EPSTEIN, *Matthias Erzberger and the Dilemma of German Democracy* (Princeton U.P., 1959).

DAVID LLOYD GEORGE, *The Truth about Reparations and War Debts* (Heinemann, 1932).

*OTTO GESSLER, *Reichswehrpolitik in der Weimarer Zeit* (Stuttgart, DVA, 1958).

*WILHELM GROENER, *Lebenserinnerungen, Jugend, Generalstab, Weltkrieg* (Göttingen, Vandenhoeck & Rupprecht, 1957).

D. GROENER-GEYER, *General Groener. Soldat und Staatsmann* (Frankfurt-M, Societäts-Verlag, 1954).

Adolf Hitler

ALAN BULLOCK, *Hitler, a Study in Tyranny* (Penguin, 1962).

A. HITLER, *Mein Kampf* (Jubiläumsausgabe, Munich, Zentralverlag der NSDAP, 1939).

— *Hitler's Secret Conversations 1941–44* (New York, Signet, 1961).

HERMANN RAUSCHNING, *Hitler Speaks* (Butterworth, 1939).

Hindenburg

*A. DORPALEN, *Hindenburg and the Weimar Republic* (Princeton U.P., 1964).

W. GÖRLITZ, *Hindenburg: Ein Lebensbild* (Bonn, Athenäum-Verlag, 1953).

WILHELM HOEGNER, *Der schwierige Aussenseiter. Erinnerungen eines Abgeordneten, Emigranten und Ministerpräsidenten* (Munich, Isar, 1959).

W. HUBATSCH, *Hindenburg und der Staat. Aus den Papieren des Generalfeldmarschalls und Reichspräsidenten von 1878 bis 1934* (Göttingen, Berlin, etc., Musterschmidt, 1966).

JAMES JOLL, *Intellectuals in Politics: Three Biographical Essays* (Essay on Rathenau) (Weidenfeld & Nicolson, 1960).

H. KESSLER, *Walther Rathenau, His Life and Work* (Gerald Howe, 1929).

GEORG KOTOWSKI, *Friedrich Ebert. Eine politische Biographie* (Wiesbaden, Franz Stein, 1963).

HANS LUTHER, *Politiker ohne Partei. Erinnerungen* (Stuttgart, DVA, 1960).

O. MEISSNER, *Staatssekretär unter Ebert–Hindenburg–Hitler* (Hamburg, Hoffmann & Campe, 1950).

HANS MEIER-WELCKER, *Seeckt* (Frankfurt-M., Bernard und Graefe, 1967).

R. MÜLLER, *Vom Kaiserreich zur Republik* (Vienna, Malik Verlag, 1924).

J. P. NETTL, *Rosa Luxemburg*, 2 vols. (Oxford U.P., 1966).

GUSTAV NOSKE, *Von Kiel bis Kapp* (Berlin, Verlag für Politik und Wirtschaft, 1920).

— *Erlebtes aus Aufstieg und Niedergang der deutschen Sozialdemokratie* (Offenbach, Bollwerk Verlag, 1947).

FRANZ VON PAPEN, *Memoirs*, tr. B. Connell (André Deutsch, 1952).

HERMANN PÜNDER, *Politik in der Reichskanzlei. Aufzeichnungen* (ed. Th. Vogelsang) (Stuttgart, DVA, 1961).

F. VON RABENAU, *Seeckt. Aus seinem Leben 1918–1936* (Leipzig, Hase & Koehler, 1940).

WALTHER RATHENAU, *Tagebuch 1907–1922* (ed.) H. Pogge-von-Strandmann (Düsseldorf, Droste, 1967).

HJALMAR SCHACHT, *The Stabilization of the Mark* (Allen & Unwin, 1927).

— *My First Seventy-Six Years* (Wingate, 1965).

PHILIPP SCHEIDEMANN, *The Making of the New Germany. The Memoirs of Philipp Scheidemann*, 2 vols., tr. J. Mitchell (New York, Appleton, 1929).

— *Der Zusammenbruch* (Berlin, Verlag für Sozialwissenschaft, 1921).

HELMUT J. SCHORR, *Adam Stegerwald. Gewerkschaftler und Politiker in der Ersten Deutschen Republik* (Recklinghausen, Kommunalverlag, 1966).

*CARL SEVERING, *Mein Lebensweg*, 2 vols. (Cologne, Greven, 1950).

GUSTAV STRESEMANN, *Vermächtnis des Nachlasses in drei Bänden*, 3 vols. (ed.) H. Bernhard (Berlin, Ullstein Verlag, 1932–3).

EARL OF SWINTON, *Sixty Years of Power* (Hutchinson, 1966).

ANNELISE THIMME, *Gustav Stresemann* (Hanover and Frankfurt-M, Worldeutsche Verlags-Anstalt, 1957).

J. W. WHEELER-BENNETT, *Hindenburg. The Wooden Titan* (Macmillan, 1936).

3. SECONDARY WORKS

*W. S. ALLEN, *The Nazi Seizure of Power. The Experience of a Single German Town 1930–1935* (Eyre & Spottiswoode, 1966).

WILLIBALT APELT, *Geschichte der Weimarer Verfassung* (Munich, Biederstein, 1946).

ALFRED ANDERLE, *Die Deutsche Rapallo-Politik* (E. Berlin, Rütten & Loening, 1962).

J. W. ANGELL, *The Recovery of Germany* (Yale U.P., 1929).

*WERNER T. ANGRESS, *Stillborn Revolution. The Communist Bid for Power in Germany. 1921–1923* (Princeton U.P., 1963).

G. AXHAUSEN, *Organisation Escherich. Die Bewegung zur Nationalen Einheit* (Berlin, Weicher, 1921).

*EDWARD W. BENNETT, *Germany and the Diplomacy of the Financial Crisis* (Harvard U.P., 1962).

*V. R. BERGHAHN, *Der Stahlhelm. Bund der Frontsoldaten* (Düsseldorf, Droste, 1966).

Carl BERGMANN, *Der Weg der Reparationen. Von Versailles über den Dawesplan zum Ziel* (Frankfurt-M, Frankfurter Societäts-Druckerei, 1926).

A. J. BERLAU, *The German Social Democratic Party 1914–1921* (New York, 1949).

W. BESSON, *Württemberg und die deutsche Staatskrise 1928–1933* (Stuttgart, DVA, 1959).

GEORGES BONNIN, *Le Putsch de Hitler a Munich en 1923* (Paris, Les Sables D'Olonne, 1966).

*KARL ERICH BORN, *Die deutsche Bankenkrise 1931* (Munich, Piper, 1967).

*K. D. BRACHER, *Die Auflösung der Weimarer Republik. Eine Studie zum Problem des Machtverfalls in der Demokratie* (Villingen, Ring Verlag, 4th edn., 1964).

— *Deutschland zwischen Demokratie und Diktatur* (Bern–Munich–Vienna, Schutz Verlag, 1964).

*— W. SAUER and G. SCHULZ, *Die Nationalsozialistische Machtergreifung*, 2nd ed. (Cologne and Opladen, Westdeutscher Verlag, 1962).

W. L. Bretton, *Stresemann and the Revision of Versailles* (Stanford U.P., 1953).

*M. Broszat, *Der Nationalsozialismus. Weltanschauung, Programm und Wirklichkeit* (Stuttgart, DVA, 1960).

*F. L. Carsten, *The Reichswehr and Politics 1918–1933* (Oxford U.P., 1966).

Norman Cohn, *Warrant for Genocide: The Myth of the Jewish World-conspiracy and the Protocols of the Elders of Zion* (Eyre & Spottiswoode, 1967).

*W. Conze and H. Raupach (eds.), *Die Staats- und Wirtschaftskrise des Deutschen Reiches 1929–33* (Stuttgart, Klett, 1967).

Gordon A. Craig, *The Politics of the Prussian Army 1640–1945* (Oxford U.P., 1955).

*— and Felix Gilbert, *The Diplomats* (Princeton U.P., 1953).

Wilfried Daim, *Der Mann, der Hitler die Ideen gab* (Munich, Isar, 1958).

Ernst Deuerlein, *Der Hitlerputsch. Bayerische Dokumente zum 9. November 1923* (Stuttgart, DVA, 1962).

Pius Dirr, *Bayerische Dokumente zum Kriegsausbruch und zum Versailler Schuldspruch* (Munich, Mühlthaler, 1922).

Wolfgang Elben, *Das Problem der Kontinuität in der deutschen Revolution 1918–1919* (Düsseldorf, Droste, 1965).

K. D. Erdmann, *Adenauer in der Rheinlandpolitik* (Stuttgart, Klett, 1966).

Johannes Erger, *Der Kapp–Lüttwitz-Putsch* (Düsseldorf, Droste, 1967).

Fritz Ernst, *The Germans and Their Modern History*, tr. C. M. Pruch (New York and London, Columbia U.P., 1966).

T. Eschenburg et al., *The Road to Dictatorship: Germany 1918–1933*, tr. L. Wilson (Wolff, 1964).

Gottfried Feder, *Der Deutsche Staat auf Nationaler und Sozialer Grundlage. Neue Wege im Staat, Finanz und Wirtschaft* (Munich, Deutschvölkische, Verlags-Buchhandlung, 1923).

G. D. Feldman, *Army, Industry and Labor in Germany 1914–1918* (Princeton U.P., 1966).

*Ossip K. Flechtheim, *Die Kommunistische Partei Deutschlands in der Weimarer Republik* (Offenbach, Bollwerk Verlag, 1948).

Georg Franz-Willing, *Die Hitlerbewegung. Der Ursprung 1919–1922* (Hamburg and Berlin, Decker, 1962).

G. Freund, *Unholy Alliance* (Chatto & Windus, 1957).

H. W. Gatzke, *Stresemann and the Rearmament of Germany* (Baltimore, Johns Hopkins, 1954).

D. J. Goodspeed, *Ludendorff. Soldier: Dictator: Revolutionary* (Hart-Davis, 1966).

Harold J. Gordon, *The Reichswehr and the German Republic 1919–1926* (Princeton U.P., 1957).

Oron J. Hale, *The Captive Press in the Third Reich* (Princeton U.P., 1964).

*W. Hartenstein, *Die Anfänge der Deutschen Volkspartei* (Düsseldorf, Droste, 1963).

*R. Heberle, *Landbevölkerung und Nationalsozialismus. Eine soziologische Untersuchung der politischen Willensbildung in Schleswig-Holstein 1918–1932* (Stuttgart, DVA, 1962).

Helmut Heiber, *Die Republik von Weimar* (Munich, DTV, 1966).

H. Helbig, *Die Träger der Rapallo-Politik* (Göttingen, Windhoeck, 1958).

A. Hermans and T. Schieder (eds.), *Staat, Wirtschaft und Politik in der Weimarer Republik. Festschrift für Heinrich Brüning* (Berlin, Duncker & Humblot, 1967).

*Lewis Hertzmann, *DNVP. Right-wing Opposition in the Weimar Republic* (Nebraska U.P., 1963).

G. Hilger and A. G. Meyer, *The Incompatible Allies, German-Soviet Relations, 1918–1941* (New York, Macmillan, 1953).

Wilhelm Hoegner, *Die verratene Republik, Geschichte der deutschen Gegenrevolution* (Munich, Isar, 1958).

H. H. Hofmann, *Der Hitlerputsch. Krisenjahre deutscher Geschichte* (Munich, Nymphenburger Verlag, 1961).

*Richard N. Hunt, *German Social Democracy 1918–1933* (New Haven, Yale U.P., 1964).

J. M. (Lord) Keynes, *The Economic Consequences of the Peace* (Macmillan, 1920).

*EBERHARD KOLB, *Die Arbeiterräte in der deutschen Innenpolitik, 1918–1919* (Düsseldorf, Droste, 1962).

G. KROLL, *Von der Weltwirtschaftskrise zur Staatskonjunktur* (Berlin, Duncker und Humblot, 1958).

A. KRUCK, *Geschichte des Alldeutschen Verbandes 1890–1939* (Wiesbaden, Steiner, 1954).

W. Z. LAQUEUR, *Russia and Germany. A Century of Conflict* (Weidenfeld & Nicolson, 1965).

G. LEWY, *The Catholic Church in Nazi Germany* (Weidenfeld & Nicolson, 1964).

W. LIEBE, *Die Deutschnationale Volkspartei* (Düsseldorf, Droste, 1956).

*A. LUCKAU, *The German Delegation at the Paris Peace Conference* (New York, Columbia U.P., 1941).

*ROLF E. LUKE, *Von der Stabilisierung zur Krise* (Zürich, Polygraphischer Verlag, 1958).

*WERNER MASER, *Die Frühgeschichte der NSDAP* (Frankfurt-M, Athenäum, 1965).

*E. MATTHIAS and R. MORSEY, *Das Ende der Parteien* (Düsseldorf, Droste, 1960).

*ALFRED MILATZ, *Wähler und Wahlen in der Weimarer Republik* (Bonn, Bundeszentrale für politische Bildung: Raiffeisendruckerei, 1965).

ALLEN MITCHELL, *Revolution in Bavaria, 1918–1919. The Eisner Regime and the Soviet Republic* (Princeton U.P., 1965).

*R. MORSEY, *Die deutsche Zentrumspartei 1917–1923* (Düsseldorf, Droste, 1966).

GEORGE L. MOSSE, *The Crisis of German Ideology. Intellectual Origins of the Third Reich* (Weidenfeld & Nicolson, 1966).

ERNST NOLTE, *Three Faces of Fascism* (Weidenfeld & Nicolson, 1965).

P. VON OERTZEN, *Die Betriebsräte in der Novemberrevolution* (Düsseldorf, Droste, 1965).

J. PETZOLD, *Die Dolchstosslegende. Eine Geschichtsfälschung im Dienst des deutschen Imperialismus und Militarismus*, 3rd ed. (E. Berlin, Akademie Verlag, 1963).

*EUGEN PRAGER, *Geschichte der USPD. Entstehung und Entwicklung der Unabhängigen Sozialdemokratischen Partei Deutschlands*, 2nd ed. (Berlin, Freiheit Verlag, 1921).

P. G. J. PULZER, *The Rise of Political Anti-semitism in Germany and Austria* (New York, John Wiley, 1964).

E. M. ROBERTSON, *Hitler's Pre-war Policy and Military Plans 1933–39* (Longmans, 1963).

*KARL ROHE, *Das Reichsbanner Schwarz-Rot-Gold* (Düsseldorf, Droste, 1966).

*E. A. ROLOFF, *Bürgertum und Nationalsozialismus 1930–1933. Braunschweigs Weg ins Dritte Reich* (Hanover, Verlag für Literatur und Zeitgeschehen, 1961).

H. R. RUDIN, *Armistice 1918* (New Haven, Yale U.P., 1944).

*WOLFGANG RUNGE, *Politik und Beamtentum im Parteienstaat. Die Demokratisierung der politischen Beamten in Preussen zwischen 1918 und 1933* (Stuttgart, Klett, 1965).

*A. J. RYDER, *The German Revolution of 1918. A Study of German Socialism in War and Revolt* (Cambridge U.P., 1967).

F. SCHADE, *Kurt Eisner und die bayerische Sozialdemokratie* (Hanover, Verlag für Literatur und Zeitgeschehen, 1961).

O. E. SCHÜDDEKOPF, *Linke Leute von Rechts* (Stuttgart, Kohlhammer, 1960).

*GERHARD SCHULZ, *Zwischen Demokratie und Diktatur* (Berlin, Gruyter, 1963).

KARL SCHWEND, *Bayern zwischen Monarchie und Diktatur* (Munich, Pflaum, 1954).

K. SONTHEIMER, *Anti-demokratisches Denken in der Weimarer Republik, Die politischen Ideen des deutschen Nationalismus* (Munich, Nymphenburger Verlag, 1962).

G. STOLTENBERG, *Politische Strömungen im schleswigholsteinischen Landvolk 1918–1933* (Düsseldorf, Droste, 1933).

R. STUCKEN, *Die deutsche Geld- und Kreditpolitik 1914–1963*, 3rd edn. (Tübingen, J. C. B. Mohr, 1964).

A. J. P. TAYLOR, *The Origins of the Second World War* (Penguin, 1964).

F. TOBIAS, *Der Reichstagsbrand. Legende und Wirklichkeit* (Rastatt, Grote, 1962).

W. TORMIN, *Zwischen Rätediktatur und sozialer Demokratie* (Düsseldorf, Droste, 1954).

*H. A. TURNER, *Gustav Stresemann and the Politics of the Weimar Republic* (Princeton U.P., 1963).

J. VARAIN, *Freie Gewerkschaften, Sozialdemokratie und Staat. Die Politik der Generalkommission unter der Führung von Carl Legien (1890–1920)* (Düsseldorf, Droste, 1956).

*THILO VOGELSANG, *Reichswehr, Staat und NSDAP* (Stuttgart, DVA, 1962).

R. G. L. WAITE, *Vanguard of Nazism. The Free Corps Movement in Postwar Germany 1918–1923* (Harvard U.P., 1952).

ERIC WALDMAN, *The Spartakist Uprising of 1919* (Milwaukee, Marquette U.P., 1958).

E. WEILL-RAYNAL, *Les Reparations Allemandes et la France*, 3 vols. (Paris, Nouvelles Éditions Latines, 1947).

J. W. WHEELER-BENNETT, *Brest-Litovsk. The Forgotten Peace March 1918* (Macmillan, 1936).

— *Nemesis of Power. The German Army in Politics 1918–1945*, 2nd ed. (Macmillan, 1964).

— *The Wreck of Reparations* (Allen & Unwin, 1933).

Z. A. B. ZEMAN, *Nazi Propaganda* (O.U.P., 1964).

LUDWIG ZIMMERMANN, *Deutsche Aussenpolitik in der Ära der Weimarer Republik* (Göttingen, Musterschmidt, 1958).

4. ARTICLES

(I have confined this list to articles cited in footnotes. They are given here in order of appearance in the text.)

WILHELM DEIST, 'Seekriegsleitung und Flottenrebellion 1918', in *Vierteljahrshefte für Zeitgeschichte*, October 1966.

LORD BRAND, 'How a Banker Watched History Happen', in *The Observer*, 8 January 1961.

FRITZ DICKMANN, 'Die Kriegsschuldfrage auf der Friedenskonferenz von Paris 1919', in *Historische Zeitschrift*, August 1963.

IMANUEL GEISS, 'The Outbreak of the First World War and German War Aims', in *The Journal of Contemporary History*, vol. 1, no. 3, 1966.

K. D. ERDMANN, 'Deutschland, Rapallo und der Westen', in *Vierteljahrshefte für Zeitgeschichte*, April 1963.

R. C. WILLIAMS, 'Russians in Germany: 1900–1914', in *The Journal of Contemporary History*, vol. I, no. 4, 1966.

ERNST DEUERLEIN, 'Hitlers Eintritt in die Politik und in die Reichswehr', in *Vierteljahrshefte für Zeitgeschichte*, April 1959.

R. H. PHELPS, 'Hitler als Parteiredner im Jahre 1920', in *Vierteljahrshefte für Zeitgeschichte*, 1963, pp. 274–330.

DIETRICH O. ORLOW, 'The Organizational History and Structure of the NSDAP, 1919–1923', in *Journal of Modern History*, June 1965.

HANS W. GATZKE, 'The Stresemann Papers', in *Journal of Modern History*, 1954, pp. 49 ff.

M. STÜRMER, 'Probleme der parlamentarischen Mehrheitsbildung in der Stabilisierungsphase der Weimarer Republik', in *Politische Vierteljahrsschrift*, Heft 1, 1967.

ATTILA CHANADY, 'The Disintegration of the German National People's Party, 1924–1930', in *Journal of Modern History*, March 1967.

H. HAMMER, 'Die deutschen Ausgaben von Hitlers "Mein Kampf" ', in *Vierteljahreshefte für Zeitgeschichte*, April 1956.

H. TREVOR-ROPER, 'Hitlers Kriegsziele', in *Vierteljahrshefte für Zeitgeschichte*, April 1960.

J. NOAKES, 'Conflict and Development in the NSDAP 1924–1927', in *Journal of Contemporary History*, October 1966.

HEINRICH BRÜNING, 'Ein Brief', in *Deutsche Rundschau*, July 1947.

K. O. VON ARETIN, 'Prälat Kaas, Franz von Papen und das Reichskonkordat von 1933', in *Vierfeljahreshefte für Zeitgeschichte*, July 1966.

Index